THE
HELICOPTER
PILOT'S MANUAL

VOLUME 1 Principles of Flight and Helicopter Handling

THE
HELICOPTER
PILOT'S MANUAL

VOLUME 1 | **Principles of Flight and Helicopter Handling**

Norman Bailey

Airlife
England

Copyright © Norman Bailey 1996

This edition published in the UK in 1996
by Airlife Publishing Ltd
First published in 1992

British Library Cataloguing in Publication Data

A catalogue record for this book
is available from the British Library

ISBN 1 85310 759 X

Printed in England by Livesey Ltd, Shrewsbury

Airlife Publishing Ltd

101 Longden Road, Shrewsbury, SY3 9EB, England

CONTENTS

1

THE PRINCIPLES OF FLIGHT

THE LIFTING FORCE
OF THE ROTOR

Helicopters and other related rotary wing aircraft are widely varied in their concept and configuration. These notes relate primarily to the single rotor helicopter of the type that employs a compensating tail rotor.

Although the aerodynamics of the helicopter are based on the same laws that govern the flight of a fixed wing aeroplane, the significance of some considerations is somewhat changed.

Both rely on lift produced from air flowing around an aerofoil, but whereas the aeroplane must move bodily through the air, the helicopter's 'wings' move independently of the fuselage and can produce lift with the aircraft remaining stationary (Hovering).

DEFINITIONS

Before examining more considerations it is necessary to define some terms that relate strictly to rotary wing flight.

a) **Plane of Rotation.** Normal to axis of rotation and parallel to the tip rotor path plane.

b) **Axis of Rotation.** An actual or imaginary line about which a body rotates. The plane of rotation is at right angles to the axis of rotation.

c) **Tip Path Plane.** Path described by the tips of the rotor blades.

d) **Rotor Disc.** The area contained by the tips of the rotor blades in flight.

e) **Pitch Angle.** The angle between the chord line of a rotor blade and the plane of rotation.

f) **Angle of Attack.** The angle between the chord line of a rotor blade and the relative airflow.

g) **Coning Angle.** The angle between the spanwise length of a blade and the blade's tip path plane.

h) **Total Rotor Thrust.** The sum of the lift of all the blades.

i) **Feathering.** The angular movement of a rotor blade about its longitudinal axis.

j) **Flapping.** The angular movement of a rotor blade about a horizontal axis. In fully articulated rotors the individual blades are free to flap about their flapping hinge.

k) **Dragging.** The angular movement of a rotor blade about an axis vertical to that rotor blade. The dragging hinge is incorporated only in fully articulated rotor systems.

l) **Coning.** Movement of the rotor blades aligning them along the resultant of centrifugal force and lift. Hence, an increase in lift would increase the coning angle, or conversely, an increase in rotor rpm would decrease the coning angle.

m) **Chord Line.** An imaginary line joining the leading edge and trailing edge of an aerofoil, which is perpendicular to the span axis.

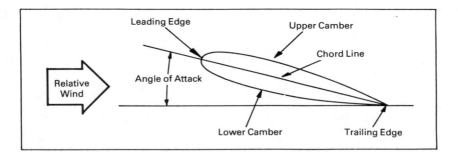

LIFT

The lift produced from the wing of an aeroplane results from a combination of many things and is commonly expressed in the formula, CL 1/2p V^{2}S.

Lift from a helicopter rotor blade can generally be expressed in the same terms but because the rotor blade moves independently of the fuselage, the velocity (V^2), when hovering in still air conditions is purely the result of the rotation of the blade.

BLADE PITCH

The wing of an aeroplane is fitted to the fuselage at some specified angle. The datums are the chord line and a line longitudinally down the fuselage. The angle between the two is known as the angle of incidence.

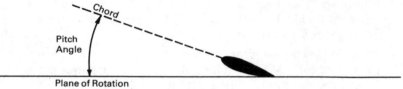

Blade Pitch.

The rotor blade, when attached to the rotor head will also have a basic setting. The datums are the chord line of the blade and the plane in which the blade is free to rotate. The angle between the two datums is known as the pitch angle.

If the blade had a constant value of pitch throughout its length, problems would arise relating to blade loading because each section of the blade would have a different rotational velocity and therefore a different value of lift. As lift is proportional to V^2, each time the speed is doubled the lift would increase fourfold.

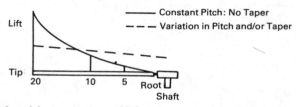

To avoid this considerable variation of lift it is necessary to increase lift at the root end and decrease some of the lift at the tip. The blade is therefore either tapered, given a washout or a combination of both. Lift from the blade will still have its greatest value near the tip but its distribution along the blade will be more uniform.

RELATIVE AIRFLOW

Consider a column of still air through which a rotor blade is moving horizontally. The effect will be to displace some of the air downwards. If a number of rotor blades are travelling along the same path in rapid succession (with a three-bladed rotor system operating at 240 rpm, a blade will be passing a given point every twelfth of a second), then the column of still air will eventually become a column of descending air.

Induced Flow.

This downwards motion of the air is known as the **induced flow**. The direction of the air relative to the blade will therefore be the resultant of the blade's horizontal travel through the air and the induced flow.

TOTAL REACTION

The force (total reaction), acting on an aerofoil can be split into components of lift and drag. Lift, at right angles to Relative Airflow, is not now providing a force in direct opposition to weight as in the case of the fixed wing aircraft. The lifting component of the total reaction must therefore be that part of which is acting along the axis of rotation. This component is known as **Rotor Thrust**.

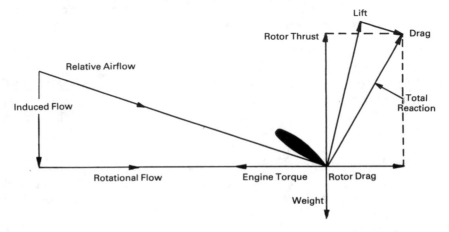

The other component of the total reaction will be in the blade's plane of rotation and is known as **Rotor Drag**.

TOTAL ROTOR THRUST

If the rotor blades are perfectly balanced and each blade is producing the same Rotor Thrust, then the **Total Rotor Thrust** can be said to be acting through the head at right angles to the plane of rotation.

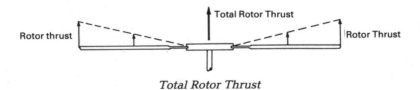

Total Rotor Thrust

CONING ANGLE

The rotor thrust will cause the blades to rise until they reach a position where their upwards movement is balanced by the outwards pull of the centrifugal force being produced by the blades rotation.

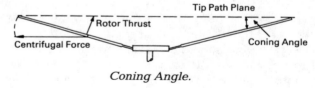

Coning Angle.

In normal operation the blades are said to be coned upwards. The **coning angle** will vary with combinations of rotor thrust and rotor rpm.

ROTOR DISC

The rotor disc is the area enclosed within the circle described by the rotor blade tips. Because this area decreases as the coning angle increases, the coning angle must never been allowed to become too big.

LIMITS OF ROTOR RPM

As centrifugal action through rotor rpm gives a measure of control of the coning angle, providing the rotor rpm are kept above a laid down minimum the coning angle will always be within safe operating limits.

There will also be upper limits to the rotor rpm due to engine and transmission considerations and end loading stresses where the blade is attached to the rotor head.

HELICOPTER SYSTEMS

INTRODUCTION

There are many variations in the design of a modern helicopter but they all share many of the major components.

FLIGHT CONTROL SYSTEMS

Main Rotor Systems

Main rotor systems are classified according to how the main rotor blades move relative to the main rotor hub.

Fully Articulated: In a fully articulated rotor system each blade is free to move up and down (flapping), back and forth (dragging) and twisting about the spanwise axis (feathering). These rotor systems normally have three or more blades.

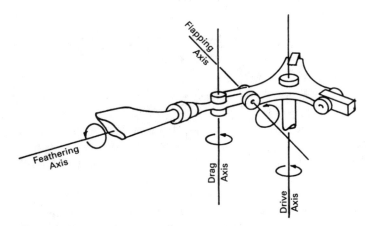

Full Articulation

Semi-rigid: this system normally uses two rotor blades rigidly attached to the main rotor hub which is free to tilt independently of the main rotor mast on what is known as a teetering hinge. This allows the blades to flap together – as one blade flaps up the other flaps down. There is no vertical hinge.

Rigid: The rigid rotor system, although mechanically simple is structurally complex because operating loads must be absorbed by bending rather than through hinges. The blades cannot flap or drag but can be feathered.

Anti-Torque Systems

Most single rotor helicopters require a separate rotor to overcome torque reaction, i.e. the tendency for the helicopter to turn in the opposite direction to that of the main rotor blades.

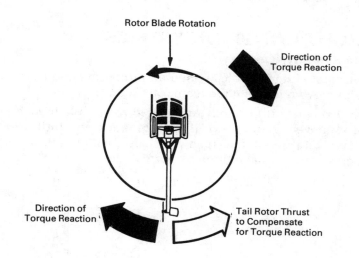

Torque Compensation.

Twin rotor helicopters do not require a separate anti-torque rotor because torque from one rotor is balanced out by the torque from the other rotor thereby cancelling out the turning tendencies.

Landing Gear

Skids: The most common type of helicopter undercarriage and suitable for landing on all types of surface. Some are fitted with dampers so that touchdown shocks are not transmitted to the main rotor system. Others absorb these shocks by allowing cross tube fittings to bend.

In order to manhandle the helicopter on the ground, small wheels are designed to be fitted into the skids and the helicopter is then raised off the ground onto the wheels so that it can then be moved by hand.

Wheels: Another common type of landing gear can be a three or four wheel configuration. Normally the nose wheel is free to swivel as the helicopter is taxied on the ground. Some types are retractable to reduce aerodynamic drag in flight.

Floats/Skis: Some helicopters are fitted with special types of landing gear such as floats for water operations or special skis for landing on snow.

Powerplant

A typical helicopter has its piston engine mounted aft and below the cabin. The engine is normally installed horizontally with a shroud around it to assist with cooling.

OPERATION OF FLIGHT CONTROL SYSTEMS

A knowledge of your flight control systems is necessary as by understanding their operation you will be able to recognize potential problems on pre-flight inspections.

Collective Pitch Control (The Lever)

Applying collective pitch indicates that the pitch angle of all the blades increases by the same amount at the same time. The lever is mechanically linked to the throttle and is the primary means of controlling power.

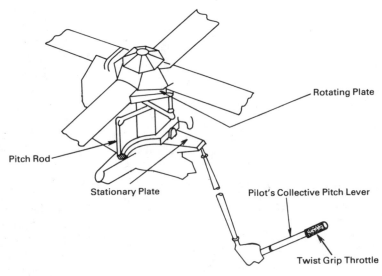

Collective pitch system.

Cyclic Pitch Control (The Stick)

The cyclic pitch control changes the pitch angle of the rotor blades in their cyclic rotation. This tilts the tip patch plane to allow forward, rearward or lateral movement of the helicopter.

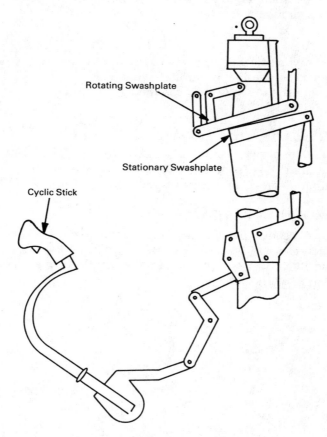

Cyclic control system.

Anti-Torque Control (The Pedals)

Because the main rotor system turns to the left the fuselage tends to turn in the opposite direction because of torque reaction. The amount of torque reaction is relative to how much power is applied to the main rotor. The tail rotor of a single rotor helicopter opposes this force and you control this anti-torque force by operating the pedals. When you apply left pedal you increase the pitch on the tail rotor blades which increases thrust to the right and moves the nose of the helicopter to the left.

Swash Plate Assembly

The purpose of a swash plate is to transmit cyclic and collective control movements to the main rotor blades. It consists of a **stationary plate** which is attached to the main rotor mast and which, although restricted from rotating, is allowed to tilt in all directions and move vertically, and a **rotating plate**. This plate is attached to the stationary plate by a bearing surface and rotates with the main rotor blades. It transmits pitch changes through mechanical linkages.

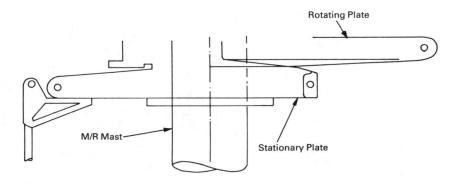

Swashplate mechanism.

Trim Systems

Most helicopters are equipped with some form of trim system to relieve you from having to hold against control forces. The neutral position of the cyclic pitch control changes as the helicopter moves off from the hover into forward flight. The control feel in a helicopter is provided mechanically and you can adjust this mechanical feel in flight by changing the neutral position of the cyclic stick.

Frictions

Since the main rotor blades tend to feed back aerodynamic forces to the pilot's controls, trim springs tend to resist any control motion. Friction controls provide adjustable resistance to control movements.

The Power Train System

On a piston engined helicopter the power train system usually consists of a clutch, main rotor transmission and drive, a tail rotor transmission and drive and a freewheel unit to allow the rotors to turn freely in the event of an engine failure.

Clutch: In an aeroplane the engine and propeller are permanently engaged but because of the greater weight of a rotor system in relation to engine power, a helicopter is usually started with the rotors disconnected from the engine. A clutch allows the engine to be started first and then gradually pick up the load of the rotor system.

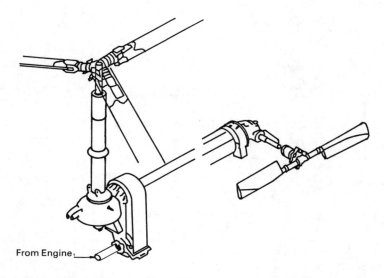

From Engine

Belt Drive: Most helicopters utilize a form of belt drive system to transmit engine power to the main rotor transmission. It normally consists of a lower pulley attached to the engine crankshaft, an upper pulley attached to the input shaft of the main transmission, an idler pulley and belt(s). Tension on the belt(s) is gradually increased to regulate the rate of rotor engagement.

Main Rotor Transmission: Transmits power from the engine to the main rotor and tail rotor. Its primary purpose is to reduce engine output RPM to the optimum rotor RPM. Helicopter transmissions are normally lubricated and cooled with their own oil supply.

Tail Rotor Drive System: A tail rotor driveshaft, powered from the main transmission, is connected to the tail rotor transmission located on the end of the tail boom. The tail rotor transmission

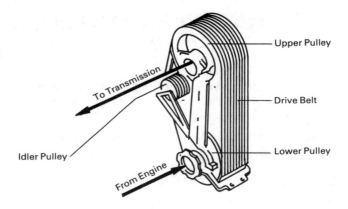

provides a right angle drive and gears to increase the input speed so that the output shaft rotates at an optimum tail rotor RPM. The tail rotor transmission is splash lubricated by its own oil supply and you can check the oil level by means of a sight glass or plug.

Freewheel Unit: All helicopters are designed so that the rotors can be disengaged from the engine in the event of a power failure. In helicopters with a belt drive system this function is provided by a one-way sprag clutch (freewheel unit), contained in the upper pulley. When the engine is driving the rotor, inclined surfaces force rollers against the outer drum. If the engine fails, the rollers move inward allowing the outer drum to continue turning.

HELICOPTER CONTROLS

A helicopter is able to climb and descend vertically, move horizontally in any direction and, whilst hovering over a spot on the ground, turn on to any selected heading.

To achieve this variety of performance the helicopter is fitted with special controls.

THE COLLECTIVE PITCH LEVER

This lever derives its name from the fact that when it is raised, it simultaneously increases the pitch angle of all the rotor blades equally. Similarly, when it is lowered, it reduces the pitch angle on all the blades equally. Such changes are termed **collective pitch movements**.

The first requirement is to be able to control the size of the total rotor thrust. We have already said that this force depends on angle of attack, airspeed and size/shape of the aerofoil. The latter two can be disregarded since they are design features. The airspeed of a rotor blade is governed by the speed of rotation which, in the present day helicopter, is virtually constant – the maximum and minimum limitations being quite close together.

Limits of Rotor RPM. The maximum rotor rpm are governed by factors such as maximum engine rpm (piston engine), and transmission limitations (gas turbine engine).

The minimum rotor rpm are normally governed by the problem of the coning angle.

Since the gap between maximum and minimum rotor rpm is so small there can be no question of using variations of rpm as a means of controlling the size of the Total Rotor Thrust and in any case, the response would be too slow because of the considerable inertia of the blades.

Pitch Angle. It follows then that the only practical means of control is by varying the angle of attack of the blades and this is done by means of the collective pitch lever. Variations in blade pitch will cause marked changes in drag and in order to maintain constant rotor rpm, changes in power must be made. This is achieved by having a throttle control on the end of the collective lever.

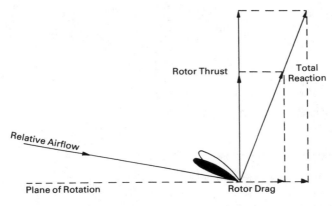

Control of Rotor RPM.

CYCLIC PITCH CONTROL

In order to move the helicopter in horizontal flight a thrust force is required which must be produced by the main rotor. This can be achieved by tilting the rotor disc so that the total rotor thrust is tilted in the direction of the required movement.

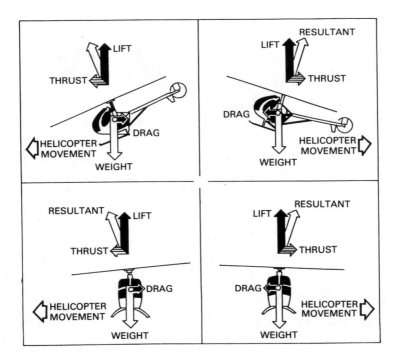

If a two bladed rotor is considered and the pitch on one blade is increased while that on the other is decreased by the same amount at the same time, then one blade will rise and the other will fall which will result in a tilt of the rotor disc.

To keep the rotor disc tilted the pitch must vary throughout the blades' 360 degrees cycle of travel. This change in pitch is known as **Cyclic Pitch** change and is achieved by the pilot moving the cyclic pitch stick.

TORQUE REACTION

Unless balanced in some way the fuselage will rotate in the opposite direction to the main rotor as a result of **Torque Reaction**. The most common method used to overcome this reaction is by fitting a tail rotor.

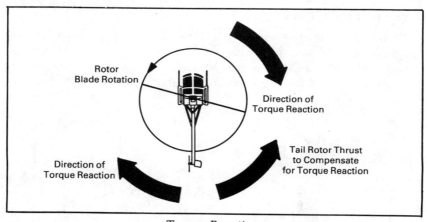

Torque Reaction.

As torque reaction is not a constant, but will vary with power changes, some means must be provided to vary the thrust of the tail rotor. This is achieved by the pilot moving yaw pedals which collectively change the pitch and thereby the angle of attack on the tail rotor blades, the pitch increasing or decreasing depending upon which pedal is moved.

When the movement of the tail rotor thrust equals the torque reaction, then the fuselage will maintain a constant direction.

ADDITIONAL TAIL ROTOR FUNCTIONS

a) **Changing heading in the Hover.** By operating the yaw pedals to produce a thrust greater or less than the torque reaction, the heading of the fuselage can be altered whilst the helicopter is hovering over a spot. The pedals operate in the correct sense in that a yaw to the right results from pushing on the right pedal and vice versa.

b) **To maintain a balanced condition in forward flight.** By using the pedals to keep the balance indicator centralized.

c) **To prevent the fuselage rotating in autorotation.** When the rotors are being turned purely by the reaction from the air and without assistance from the engine, friction will cause the fuselage to rotate in the same direction as the rotor.

Directional control is maintained by changing the pitch on the tail rotor to such a degree that the tail rotor produces thrust in a direction opposite to that when the rotor is driven by engine power.

The tail rotor blades are symmetrical in shape and must be capable of being turned to produce plus or minus values of pitch.

TAIL ROTOR DRIFT

Consider a bar which is being turned under the influence of a couple YY about a point X. The rotation will stop if a couple of equal value, ZZ, pulls in the opposite direction.

The rotation would also stop if a single force was used to produce a moment equal to the couple, YY, but there will now be a side loading on the pivot point, X.

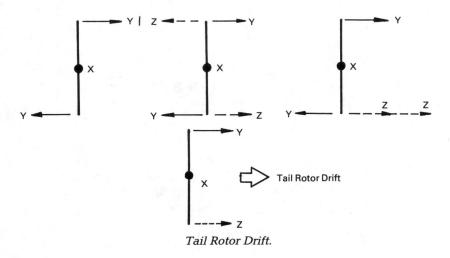

Tail Rotor Drift.

The tail rotor of a helicopter produces a moment to overcome the couple arising from torque reaction which in turn causes a side loading on the pivot point or axis of rotation of the main rotor.

This side loading is known as **Tail Rotor Drift** and unless corrected would result in the helicopter moving sideways over the ground.

Since the value of a moment is the product of FORCE x DISTANCE, the greater the distance that the tail rotor acts from the main rotor axis of rotation, the smaller the force required. In practice, the tail rotor is normally positioned just clear of the main rotor.

Tail rotor drift can be corrected for by tilting the rotor disc away from the direction of the drift. This can be achieved by:

a)   The pilot moving the cyclic pitch stick;

b)   Rigging the controls so that when the cyclic is in the centre the disc is actually tilted by the right amount;

c)   By mounting the engine so that the drive shaft to the rotor is offset;

d)   By causing the disc to tilt when the collective pitch lever is raised.

TAIL ROTOR ROLL

If the tail rotor is mounted on the fuselage below the level of the main rotor, the tail rotor drift corrective force being produced by the main rotor will create a rolling couple with the tail rotor thrust, causing the helicopter to hover one skid/wheel low.

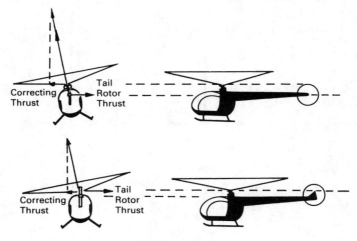

Tail Rotor Roll.

This can be overcome if the tail rotor is raised to the level of the main rotor by cranking the fuselage or fitting the tail rotor to a pylon but this condition will only be achieved if the helicopter is loaded with the C of G in the ideal position.

SHROUDED TAIL ROTOR

The conventional tail rotor operates in difficult vibratory and aerodynamic conditions and is susceptible to foreign object damage and danger to ground personnel.

One solution to this disadvantage is the shrouded tail rotor or **Fenestron**. This consists of a rotor with several small blades hinged about the feathering axis only and rotating within a shroud provided in the tail boom or fin.

ROTOR FREEDOM OF MOVEMENT

FEATHERING

This describes the movement of the blade relative to its plane of rotation. Feathering takes place as a result of changes in collective or cyclic pitch.

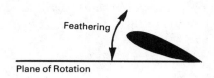

Feathering.

FLAPPING

This describes the movement of the blade perpendicular to the hub. Flapping will occur following collective and cyclic pitch changes, variations in rotor rpm and as a result of changes in the speed and direction of the airflow relative to the disc which occurs in certain in-flight conditions.

To alleviate bending stresses which would otherwise occur, the blade is allowed to flap about a flapping hinge. In some helicopters the blades are allowed to see-saw about the hub.

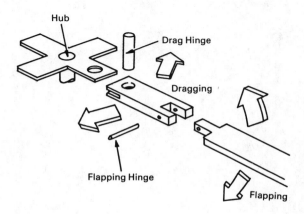

DRAGGING

This describes the freedom given to each blade to allow it to move in the plane of rotation independently of the other blades.

To avoid bending stresses at the root, the blade is allowed to drag about a dragging hinge but movement about the hinge is retarded by some form of drag damper to avoid undesirable oscillations.

Dragging occurs because of:

Periodic Drag Changes

When the helicopter moves horizontally, the blade's angle of attack is continually changing during each complete revolution to provide assymmetry of rotor thrust. This variation in angle of attack results in variation in rotor drag and consequently the blade will lead or lag about the dragging hinge.

Changing Position of the Blade C of G Relative to the Hub

Consider the helicopter stationary on the ground in still air conditions, rotors turning. The radius of the blades' C of G relative to the axis of rotation will be constant.

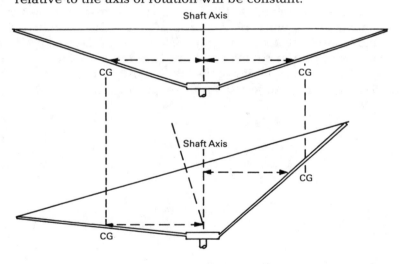

Changing Position of Blade C of G.

If the cyclic stick is moved the blade will flap up on one side of the disc and flap down on the other to produce a change in disc attitude.

With the helicopter stationary on the ground, the axis about which the blades are turning will not have altered, so the radius of the blades' C of G relative to the axis will be changing continuously through each 360 degrees of travel.

This variation in the radius will cause the blade to speed up or slow down about the dragging hinge, depending upon whether the radius is reducing or increasing. This is known as the **CORIOLIS EFFECT**.

The same effect will occur when the helicopter first moves into horizontal flight.

Hooke's Joint Effect

This effect is difficult to describe but is basically the movement of the blade to reposition itself relative to the other blades when cyclic stick is applied. Its effect is very similar to the movement of the blades' C of G relative to the hub.

Consider a rotor hovering in still air. When viewed from above the shaft axis, the blades A, B, C and D appear equally spaced relative to the shaft axis. When a cyclic tilt of the disc occurs the cone axis will have tilted but if still viewed from the shaft axis, which has not tilted, blade A will appear to increase its radius and blade C decrease its radius. Blades B and D must maintain position in order to achieve their true radial positions on the cone. If follows therefore, that they must move relative to the shaft axis and position themselves accordingly.

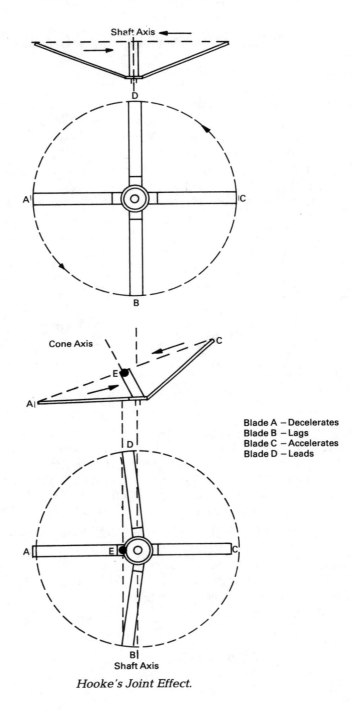

Hooke's Joint Effect.

FLAPPING TO EQUALITY

Moving the cyclic stick does not alter the magnitude of total rotor thrust but simply changes the disc attitude. This is achieved by the blades flapping to equality when the cyclic pitch change is made.

Consider a blade of a helicopter in the hover where the angle of attack is six degrees. A cyclic stick movement decreases the blade pitch and assuming that initially the direction of the relative airflow remains unchanged, the reduction in pitch will reduce both the blade's angle of attack and rotor thrust.

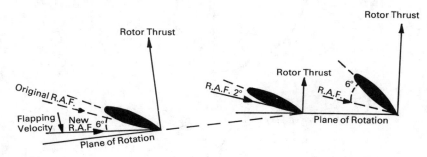

Flapping to Equality.

The blade will now begin to flap down causing an automatic increase in the blade's angle of attack. When the angle of attack is back to six degrees again, rotor thrust will return to its original value and the blade will continue to follow a path to keep the angle of attack constant. Thus cyclic pitch will alter the plane in which the blade is rotating but the angle of attack remains unchanged.

The reverse takes place when a blade experiences an increase in cyclic pitch.

Therefore any change in angle of attack through control action or in-flight conditions causes the blades to flap, and they will do so until they restore the rotor thrust – they have then **Flapped to Equality**.

PHASE LAG
AND ADVANCE ANGLE

CONTROL ORBIT

In its simplest form of operation, movement of the collective pitch lever causes a flat plate mounted centrally on the rotor shaft to rise and fall. Movement of the cyclic stick causes it to tilt, the direction of tilt being controlled by the direction in which the cyclic stick is moved.

Rods of equal length, called Pitch Operating Arms, connect the flat plate to the rotor blades.

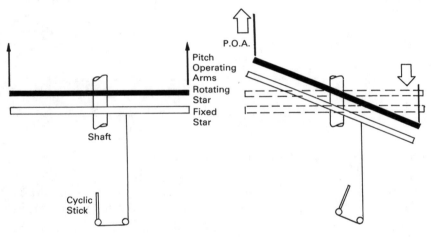

Control Orbit.

When the flat plate is tilted the pitch operating arms move up or down increasing or decreasing the pitch on the blades.

The flat plate can be more accurately described as a **Control Orbit** because it represents the plane in which the pitch operating arms are rotating.

PITCH OPERATING ARM MOVEMENT

Consider now the effect of the movement of a pitch operating arm when the control orbit has been tilted two degrees. (It is assumed that the control orbit tilts in the same direction as the stick is moved.)

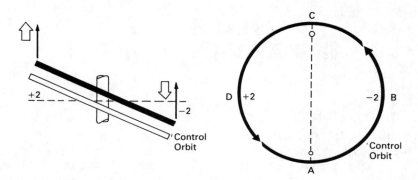

Pitch Operating Arm Movement.

If the movement of a pitch operating arm through 360 degrees of travel is plotted on a simple graph the result is as shown below.

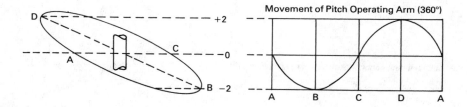

RESULTANT CHANGE IN DISC ATTITUDE

The rotor blades will respond to the cyclic pitch change by flapping and the resultant change in disc attitude can be determined by following the movement of each blade of a two bladed rotor system.

Consider the rotor blades to be positioned at A and C when the control orbit is tilted and the pitch operating arms are attached to the control orbit directly beneath the blades.

As the blade moves anti-clockwise from A it will experience a reduction in pitch and the blade will flap down. Rate of flapping varies with the amount of pitch change so the blade will be experiencing its greatest rate of flapping down as it passes position B (maximum pitch change). In the next ninety degrees of travel the pitch is returning from −2 degrees back to 0 degrees so that the Rate of flapping will have died out by position C. The blade which started at position A is flapping down for 180 degrees of travel and will therefore reach a low position at C.

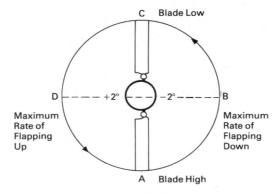

Resultant Change in Disc Attitude.

The reverse will take place with the other blade, which will reach a high position at A. The disc will now be tilted along the axis BD, ninety degrees removed from the tilt axis of the control orbit.

PHASE LAG

When cyclic pitch is applied the blades will automatically flap to equality. In doing so the disc attitude will change, the blade reaching its highest and lowest position ninety degrees later than the point when it experiences the maximum increase and decrease of cyclic pitch. The variation between the tilt of the control orbit and the subsequent tilt of the rotor is known as Phase Lag.

ADVANCE ANGLE

If the control orbit tilts in the same direction as the cyclic stick, and as a result the disc tilts ninety degrees out of phase with the control orbit, then the disc will also be tilting ninety degrees out of phase with the cyclic stick. Thus, unless the system is compensated in some way, moving the stick forward would cause the helicopter to move sideways.

One way to overcome this is to arrange for the blade to receive the maximum alteration in cyclic pitch 90 degrees before the blade is over the highest and lowest points on the control orbit.

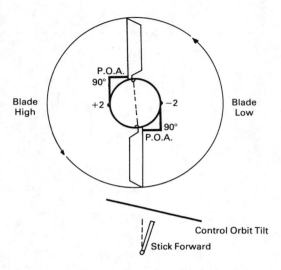

Advance Angle.

Another way would be to make the control orbit tilt so that it is out of phase with the cyclic stick by the required angle.

The angular distance that the pitch operating arm is positioned on the control orbit in advance of the blade to which it relates is known as the **Advance Angle**.

HOVERING

TAKE-OFF TO THE HOVER

To lift the helicopter off the ground a lifting force must be produced equal and opposite to the weight which is acting vertically downwards through the helicopter's centre of gravity.

When the rotor is turning at flying rpm but the collective lever is fully down, very little rotor thrust is being produced. As the collective lever is raised the blades will begin to cone up and eventually the rotor thrust will be exactly equal to the weight. If the collective lever is raised further the rotor thrust will again increase and becoming greater than weight, the helicopter will accelerate upwards.

After a short time the acceleration will become a steady rate of climb, the helicopter continuing in this state until such time as the pilot lowers the collective lever.

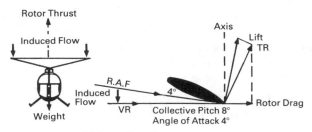

Take-off to Hover.

Consider the helicopter to be 200 feet above the ground when the collective pitch is lowered just the right amount to stop the helicopter from climbing. The helicopter will come to the hover and being well clear of the ground it is referred to as a **Free Air Hover**. To present the hover in terms of figures, consider that the four degrees is the angle of attack required to produce the necessary rotor thrust to balance the weight and that this is being achieved with, say, eight degrees of collective pitch.

VERTICAL DESCENT

From the free air hover if the collective lever is lowered the angle of attack will reduce, rotor thrust becomes less than weight and the helicopter will begin to accelerate downwards. The airflow resulting from the helicopter's descent will be opposing the induced flow and will cause the angle of attack to increase. When it again reaches four degrees, rotor thrust will equal weight and the downward acceleration will become a steady rate of descent.

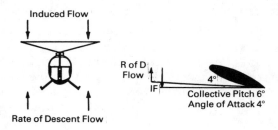

Vertical Descent.

In a vertical climb the reverse takes place. Increased pitch increases the angle of attack, rotor thrust becomes greater than weight and the helicopter accelerates upwards. The airflow from the rate of climb is in the same direction as the induced flow and the resultant change in airflow direction to the blade will gradually reduce the angle of attack.

When it again reaches four degrees, rotor thrust equals weight and the acceleration upwards will become a steady rate of climb.

GROUND EFFECT

In a free air hover the resistance to the induced flow is only the resistance of the surrounding air.

In a hover close to the ground, the ground will also resist the induced flow and be at a maximum when hovering just above the surface.

The Ground Effect intensifies the pressure differential around the rotor, the accelerated air having passed through the rotor strikes the ground and is slowed down, increasing the pressure under the rotor. This causes a reduction in the induced flow and a consequent increase in angle of attack. Therefore, the same angle of attack can be maintained in ground effect (IGE), with less collective pitch and power than required out of ground effect (OGE).

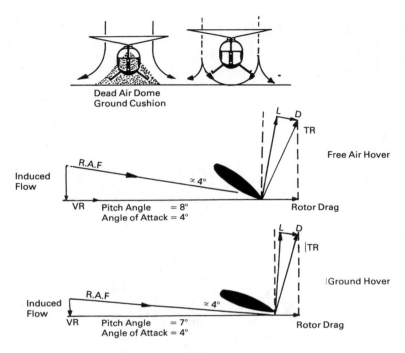

Ground Effect.

FACTORS AFFECTING THE GROUND CUSHION

a) The height the helicopter is hovering above the ground. Its effect disappears at a height equal to about three quarters of the diameter of the rotor disc.

b) Nature of the ground. (Rough ground dissipates the cushion.)

c) Slope of the ground. (Uneven ground cushion can result.)

d) Wind velocity. (The cushion is displaced downwind.)

RECIRCULATION

Whenever a helicopter is hovering close to the ground some of the air passing through the disc is recirculated and it would appear that the recirculated air increases in speed as it passes through a second time.

This local increase in induced flow near the blade tips gives rise to a loss of rotor thrust. Some recirculation is always taking place, but over a flat, even surface, the loss of rotor thrust to recirculation is more than compensated for by the ground cushion effect.

If the helicopter is hovering over long grass the loss of lift due to recirculation will increase and in some cases the effect will be greater than the ground cushion. When this situation arises, more power and collective pitch would be required to hover near the ground than to hover in free air.

Recirculation will increase when any obstruction on the surface or near to where the helicopter is hovering prevents the air from flowing evenly away. This can be dangerous, especially if it develops only on one side of the disc.

Do not hover within one rotor diameter of a building or another helicopter measured from the rotor tips.

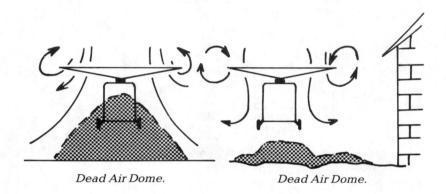

Dead Air Dome.   *Dead Air Dome.*

POWER

Power is defined as the **Rate** of doing **Work**.

Therefore $\textbf{Power} = \dfrac{\textbf{Work}}{\textbf{Time}} = \dfrac{\textbf{Drag x Distance}}{\textbf{Time}}$

But $\qquad \dfrac{\textbf{Distance}}{\textbf{Time}} = \textbf{Velocity}$

Therefore **Power = Drag x Velocity**

Power is normally expressed in terms of horsepower, one horse-power being equal to 550 feet/lbs/seconds or 33,000 feet/lbs/minute.

When an object is moved **Force** is required to overcome its resistance. If the **Force** is multiplied by the **Distance** the object is moved the product is the amount of **Work** done.

The resistance set up by the rotor blades as they turn through the air is called **Drag**. Since in any balanced equation **Force** equals **Drag** then **Work** must be equal to **Drag x Distance**.

The resistance or **Drag** of a body moving through the air will vary as the **Square** of the speed, but the **Power** required to balance the drag will vary as the **Cube** of the speed.

POWER REQUIRED

The power required to maintain level flight throughout the helicopter's speed range can be considered under three main headings.

a) **Parasite Power**. This is the power required to overcome the drag of the fuselage when the helicopter is moving in straight and level flight.

b) **Rotor Profile Power**. The power component related to the blades' speed for a fixed value of drag is known as Rotor Profile Power. The drag value will be minimum with the collective pitch lever fully down and increase as the lever is raised. However, when the main rotor is turning, ancillary equipment, drive shafts and the tail rotor will also be absorbing power. All these power requirements are **included** in calculating Rotor Profile Power.

As forward speed increases the power required to maintain

rotor rpm will increase. The reason for this is because in forward flight the increase in drag of the advancing blade will be greater than the decrease in drag of the retreating blade.

Rotor Profile Power accounts for about forty per cent of the power required to hover.

c) **Induced Power**. When the collective pitch lever is fully down there is virtually no rotor thrust being produced. In order to increase rotor thrust the lever must be raised but this will give rise to:

    i)   An increase in rotor drag.

    ii)   An increase in the mass air flowing down through the rotor disc.

In order to maintain a constant rotor rpm more power must be applied to balance the increasing drag of the blades. This increase in power is known as Induced Power because it is the extra power required to overcome the rise in drag when the blades are inducing airflow down through the rotor.

Induced power accounts for about sixty per cent of the power required to hover.

The power required to maintain the helicopter in straight and level flight at any given forward speed will be the combination of Rotor Profile Power, Induced Power and Parasite Power.

POWER AVAILABLE

The efficiency of the helicopter rotor system is taken into account in assessing the Power Required so Power Available is therefore the power available **TO** the rotor and not **FROM** the rotor.

Referring to the graph:

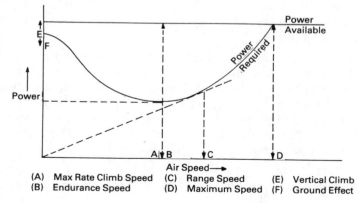

(A) Max Rate Climb Speed	(C) Range Speed	(E) Vertical Climb
(B) Endurance Speed	(D) Maximum Speed	(F) Ground Effect

The maximum forward speed will be where the two curves cross. The speed to give maximum rate of climb will be where the two curves are furthest apart, the greater the power available the faster the rate of climb. Range speed will be where a line drawn from the point of origin of the graph touches the power required curve at a tangent. (This will be true for piston engined helicopters only — range speed for gas turbine helicopters is appreciably higher.) Endurance speed will be the speed for minimum power, the lowest point on the power required curve.

FACTORS AFFECTING POWER AVAILABLE/POWER REQUIRED

Power Available

In a piston engined helicopter power available is affected by density and altitude changes. This can be compensated for by turbocharging.

Power Required

The power required by the rotor is affected by the air density and all-up weight. Consider a helicopter hovering outside ground effect. If rotor rpm are maintained as height is increased, Rotor Profile Power will decrease because of the reduction in air density. If total rotor thrust is to be maintained the collective pitch lever must be raised to compensate for this density change and therefore the Induced Power must increase, eventually leading to the total power required curve moving up the graph.

Weight

Any increase in weight will require a greater total rotor thrust and for a given rotor rpm can only be achieved by increasing collective pitch. The helicopter will therefore reach the height at which it will produce its optimum blade setting sooner than if it were lightly laden.

LIMITED POWER

Changes in air density, altitude and all-up weight will cause the power available and power required curves to move closer together. Power available may eventually be sufficient to hover only in ground effect and in extreme conditions there may be insufficient power to hover at all.

Rarely are conditions the same at the take-off and landing areas. In order that the pilot may make an assessment of the power available before committing himself to a landing, a simple in-flight power check can be carried out.

When flying straight and level at some pre-determined airspeed (usually around the 40 mph mark), a note is made of the power (manifold pressure), required. Full power is then applied whilst maintaining rotor rpm to establish maximum power available. The difference between the two readings is the power margin and it is this that determines the type of landing techniques that can safely be carried out.

A similar type of power check can be carried out in the hover before transitioning away in order to assess the helicopter's take-off capability.

These calculations do not allow for any wind effect, this being considered a bonus.

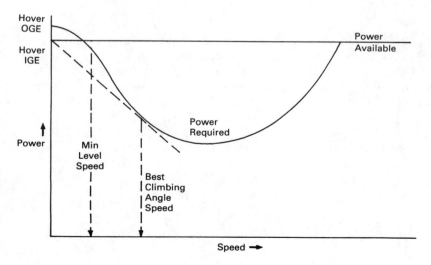

BEST CLIMBING ANGLE

When operating with limited power the helicopter must be moving forward in order to climb. In order to assess the steepest climbing angle it is necessary to find the best rate of climb/forward speed ratio.

This can be determined by drawing a line from the point where the power available curve cuts the vertical axis of the graph tangential to the power required curve. Where the two lines touch is the speed for maximum climbing angle. This point indicates the best ratio of power margin for climbing against minimum forward speed, therefore the steepest angle. It will always be less than the maximum rate of climb speed.

TURNING

As well as providing a component to balance weight and a force to maintain speed, the total rotor thrust must also supply a further component to change the direction of the helicopter in a balanced turn.

Its effect is similar to an increase in all-up weight. In a thirty degree bank turn the apparent increase in weight is fifteen per cent and in a sixty degree bank turn, 100%.

To maintain height in the turn more collective pitch is required therefore more power is used which causes the power required curve to move up the graph.

The maximum angle of bank that can be achieved by a helicopter in a level turn is that angle where the airspeed is the speed for maximum rate of climb. If the bank is increased beyond this point height will be lost and rotor rpm will decay.

OVERPITCHING

High pitch angles cause high rotor drag which means more power to maintain a constant rotor rpm. If the extra power is not available, rotor rpm will decay and the blades cone upwards. The disc area will decrease, more pitch will be required and the rotor rpm will reduce further.

This situation is called **Overpitching** and is dangerous because the only corrective action is to lower the collective lever and reduce the pitch angle, which in turn means a loss of height.

Overpitching is usually caused through mishandling the collective lever without a corresponding throttle movement. In this case throttle should be applied to restore rotor rpm and, if necessary, the collective lever should be lowered.

FORWARD FLIGHT

SYMMETRY OF ROTOR THRUST

If a helicopter is stationary on the ground in still air conditions, rotors turning, and some collective pitch is applied then the rotor thrust produced by each blade will be the same.

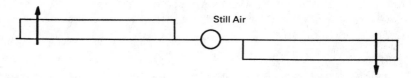

The speed of the relative airflow over each blade will be equal to the speed of rotation of the blades.

DISSYMMETRY OF ROTOR THRUST

If the conditions change and the helicopter now faces into a wind, during a blade's rotation through 360 degrees half the time it will be moving into the wind and half the time with the wind. The rotor disc can therefore be divided into the **Advancing** and **Retreating** sides.

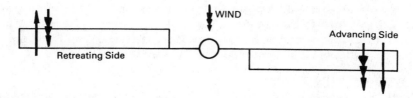

The value of rotor thrust across the disc will no longer be uniform and unless some method is employed to compensate for this the helicopter will roll towards the retreating side.

This condition where one side of the disc has more rotor thrust than the other is known as **Dissymmetry of Rotor Thrust**.

FLAPBACK

To maintain control of the helicopter it is obvious that this dissymmetry must not be allowed to take place. One method of preventing it is to decrease the angle of attack on the advancing blade and to increase it on the retreating one so that each blade produces the same value of rotor thrust. With a fully articulated rotor head this change in angle of attack takes place automatically but in so doing, results in a change of disc attitude.

As the blade begins to travel on the advancing side the relative airflow will increase. Rotor thrust increases and the blade flaps up, maximum **rate** of flapping occurring at point A.

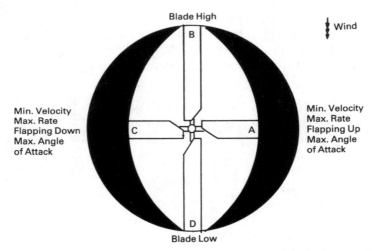

For the next ninety degrees of travel the velocity of the relative airflow begins to decrease so the **rate** of flapping decreases. When the blade reaches point B, relative airflow will have the same value as at point D, so the **rate** of flapping dies out but because the blade has been rising all the time since point D, it will reach its highest position at point B.

The reverse will take place on the retreating side, the blade having its maximum **rate** of flapping down at point C and reaching its lowest position at point D.

The rotor disc will therefore have flapped away from the wind and this change of disc attitude which has occurred without any control movement is known as **Flapback**.

FACTORS AFFECTING MAXIMUM FORWARD SPEED

Cyclic Stick Design Limits

To initiate forward flight the pilot moves the stick forward to tilt the rotor disc. The disc tilts by the same amount that the stick has been moved. As the helicopter starts to move forward, the cyclic stick has to be moved further forward again in order to overcome the effects of flapback. Thus a speed could be reached where all the cyclic stick movement has been used up to correct for flapback with nothing left to increase forward speed further.

Airflow Reversal

The speed of rotation of the retreating blade is high at the tip and low at the root. The airflow from forward flight will have an equal value for the whole length of the blade. As a result, the velocity of the relative airflow along the blade will vary and where the airflow from forward flight is greater than the blade's rotational velocity, the airflow will then be from behind the blade.

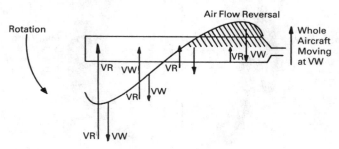

Although this does not directly affect the maximum forward speed it does mean that cyclic stick will have to be used to correct the change in disc attitude that would otherwise occur.

Retreating Blade Stall

To make up for the loss in relative speed, the blade must operate at a higher angle of attack. The maximum angle being reached when the blade is halfway round on the retreating side.

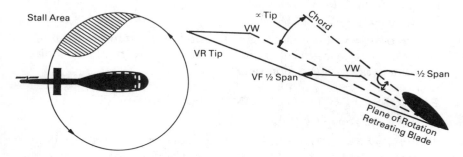

As the helicopter's forward speed increases the greater the retreating blade's angle of attack must become. Eventually a forward speed will be reached where the retreating blade will stall. The stall starting at the blade tip and spreading inboard.

Compressibility

The rotational velocity at the blade tip can be as high as 400 to 500 mph. When the helicopter is in forward flight the additional velocity over the advancing blade will increase the relative airflow by an amount equal to the forward speed. It will have a maximum effect when the advancing blade is halfway between the rear and front of the disc.

Limits of Cyclic Stick Imposed by AUW, Altitude & C of G

The more heavily the helicopter is loaded the greater must be the angle of attack to produce the necessary rotor thrust. The retreating blade will therefore reach its stalling angle at a lower forward speed with a higher all-up weight than when it is lightly laden. As forward speed is a function of cyclic stick there will be a limit on the movement of the stick imposed by the speed at which the retreating blade will stall.

To hover a helicopter at altitude requires a greater angle of attack because of the reduced air density. In forward flight the situation becomes the same as for an increase in all-up weight.

Also in the hover, the attitude of the fuselage is determined by the position of the centre of gravity. The further aft it is the more tail down the attitude and greater must become the forward movement of the cyclic stick to keep the helicopter stationary. Consequently, less cyclic stick is available for forward flight. The situation is reversed when the centre of gravity is too far forward.

CHARACTERISTICS OF BLADE STALL

Retreating blade stall can be experienced as a result of high forward speed, flying in turbulence, making abrupt or excessive control movements and carrying out manoeuvres with high G loading.

The approach of retreating blade stall can be detected by rotor roughness, erratic stick forces and stick shake. If these conditions are ignored a pitch up tendency will develop followed by a roll towards the retreating side of the rotor disc.

Recovery action is to reduce forward speed, reduce collective pitch, reduce the severity of the manoeuvre or by combining the above actions together.

INFLOW ROLL

As previously stated, the effect of air moving horizontally across the rotor disc will reduce the induced flow. However, this reduction is not uniform because air passing across the disc is being continuously pulled down by the action of the rotor blades. This means that air moving horizontally towards the disc will cause the greatest reduction in induced flow at the front of the disc and the smallest reduction at the rear.

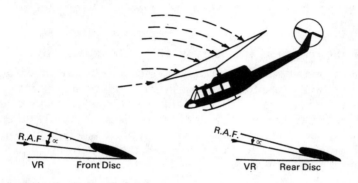

This overall reduction in induced flow will cause an increase in rotor thrust, but because the increase in angle of attack is not uniform the disc will roll towards the advancing side.

Inflow roll will have its greatest effect at low speed and the axis about which the rotor disc will tilt will vary with forward speed. Most helicopters therefore require the cyclic stick to move forward and towards the retreating side in forward flight.

GROUND RESONANCE

Ground resonance can be defined as being a vibration of large amplitude resulting from a forced or self-induced vibration to a mass in contact with or resting upon the ground.

The helicopter pilot will recognise ground resonance from a rocking motion of the fuselage and, if early corrective action is not taken, the amplitude can increase to a point where it will become uncontrollable and the helicopter will roll over.

CAUSES OF GROUND RESONANCE

If an object is vibrating at its natural frequency it will continue or damp out depending on the source of the vibration. If a second vibration is present of the same frequency it will amplify the original vibration and the object can then resonate to destruction.

Two vibrations are therefore necessary for resonance to occur.

The initial vibration which causes ground resonance can already be present in the rotor head before the helicopter comes into contact with the ground. Ideally, the rotor disc should have its centre of gravity over the centre of rotation but, if for any reason its position is displaced, then a 'wobble' will develop. This would have an effect similar to an unbalanced flywheel rotating at speed.

Ground resonance can also be induced by the undercarriage being in light contact with the ground, particularly if the frequency of oscillation of the oleos/tyres is in sympathy with the rotor head vibration.

Rotor Head Vibration

Rotor blades should be correctly balanced at manufacture but flight in icing conditions can cause an unbalance with uneven accumulation of ice on them. Moisture absorption can be another cause of unbalance. Pre-flight inspection should always include a check to see that the rotor blade drain holes are unblocked.

On a three-bladed rotor system the blades should be equally spaced 120 degrees apart. If a drag damper is sticking then the centre of gravity of the rotor will be displaced away from the axis of rotation.

A rotor which is greatly out of track may set up an unbalanced condition which will be transmitted through the helicopter. This type of unbalance results in nothing more than a 'rough' helicopter. If enough unbalance exists it is possible that a combination of factors may be encountered that would result in ground resonance being induced.

Vibrations can also be caused through mishandling (overcontrolling) the cyclic stick during landing, operating with incorrect or different oleo/tyre pressures, and taxying/running take-offs/run-on landings over rough ground.

RECOVERY ACTION

If flying rpm are available — **Lift Off immediately**. (Flying rpm should always be maintained until the landing has been completed.)

Land immediately if flying rpm are not available or if take-off is not practicable, lower lever fully and reduce power, brakes on, switch off.

VORTEX RING

Although vortices are always present around the edge of the rotor, under certain airflow conditions they will intensify and, coupled with a stall spreading outwards from the blade root, result in a sudden loss of rotor thrust and a subsequent rapid loss of height.

This condition is similar in some ways to stalling in a fixed wing aeroplane and when it occurs the helicopter is said to be in a state of Vortex Ring.

CAUSES

This state can be entered from more than one manoeuvre but the airflow conditions which cause it to occur remain the same. Vortex Ring can only occur when **all** of the following are present:

a) **Power On** (giving an induced flow down through the disc)

b) **High Rate of Descent** (produces an external airflow directly opposing the induced flow)

c) **Low Forward Speed**

DEVELOPMENT

When the helicopter is hovering in still air conditions the direction of the relative airflow can be determined from the blades' rotational speed and the induced flow, both of which will have their greatest value near the tip of the blade but because of washout, the root end will have the greatest angle of attack.

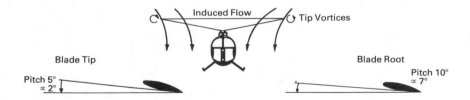

Consider the effect of reducing the collective pitch to commence a rate of descent. When the descent is established a new airflow component will exist directly opposing the induced flow which in turn will alter the direction of the relative airflow along the blade.

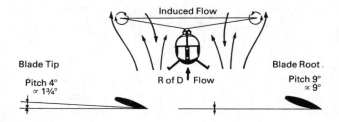

At the root end the airflow from the rate of descent is opposing the induced flow, thereby increasing the angle of attack.

In the area of the blade tip the upflow of air joins and intensifies the tip vortices, increases the induced flow and reduces the angle of attack.

If the collective pitch lever is lowered further the rate of descent will increase, the process above will be repeated and eventually a condition will be reached where the root end of the blade will reach its stalling angle. At this stage, rotor thrust is decreasing both at the blade tip due to the vortices and at the blade root because of the stalled condition, leaving an area in between to produce the rotor thrust necessary to balance weight.

Any further lowering of the collective lever results in a higher rate of descent which will reduce the area of the rotor blade that is effectively producing rotor thrust and, once a condition is reached where rotor thrust becomes insufficient to balance weight, the rate of descent will rapidly increase.

Wind tunnel experiments have shown that tip vortices form and intensify in a most erratic manner. Dissymmetry of rotor thrust occurs and the helicopter will pitch, roll and yaw to no set pattern making control extremely difficult.

In the fully developed Vortex Ring state, raising the collective pitch lever will only aggravate the condition and instead of reducing the rate of descent will actually cause it to increase.

The higher the all-up weight of the helicopter the higher will be the collective pitch setting to maintain height. Consequently, Vortex Ring state can occur at an earlier stage if the helicopter is operating at higher all-up weights than when it is lightly laden.

SYMPTOMS

Judder and cyclic stick shake

Random yawing, rolling and pitching

Rapid increase in rate of descent

RECOVERY

To recover from a state of Vortex Ring it is necessary to change the airflow conditions which cause it.

The recommended technique is to apply forward cyclic stick to change the disc attitude and gain a higher forward speed so that the rate of descent flow no longer opposes the induced flow. Then wait until there is a positive increase in indicated airspeed before applying power.

Another method is to enter autorotation, but the resulting considerable height loss by the time a full recovery is made has to be taken into consideration.

The pilot should therefore avoid the situations likely to cause Vortex Ring by restricting his rate of descent when his airspeed is low. The most likely flight conditions where this will occur will usually be within 500 feet of the ground when recovery techniques are unlikely to be successful.

AUTOROTATION

Under normal flight conditions the rotor drag is overcome with engine power. When an engine malfunctions or is deliberately disengaged from the rotor system some other force must be used to maintain the rotor rpm.

This is done by lowering the collective pitch lever fully and allowing the helicopter to descend so that the relative airflow approaches the blades in such a manner that the airflow itself provides the driving force.

Under these conditions the helicopter is said to be in a state of **Autorotation**.

Although most autorotations are carried out with forward speed, the explanation as to why the blade continues to turn can best be seen if it is considered that the helicopter is autorotating vertically in still air. Under these conditions if the various forces involved are calculated for one blade they will be valid for all the other blades irrespective of where they are during their 360 degrees of travel.

The various angles and airflows which will be referred to are shown below.

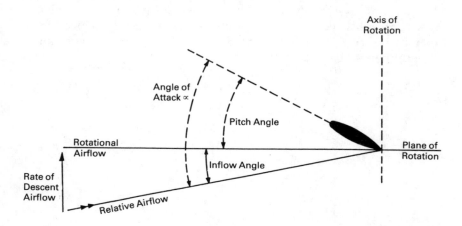

It can be seen that the inflow angle has been determined from the blade's rotational velocity and the airflow caused by the rate of descent.

AUTOROTATIVE FORCE/ ROTOR DRAG

If we consider three sections of a rotor blade — A, B and C — the direction of the relative airflow for each section can then be determined from the blade's rpm and the helicopter's rate of descent.

The rate of descent will have a common value for each section but the rotational velocity will decrease from the blade tip towards the root, therefore the inflow angle must be progressively increasing. Because of the washout incorporated in the blade the pitch angle is also increasing and as the blade's angle of attack is the pitch angle plus the inflow angle, the blade's maximum angle of attack will be at the root.

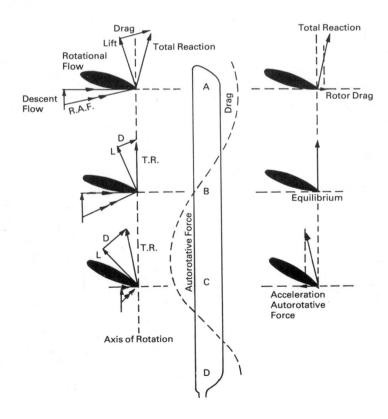

If the angle of attack for each section of the blade is known, then by referring to aerofoil data tables the position of the **Total Reaction** can be determined and the vectors of rotor thrust and rotor drag located.

At section A the condition is the same as for powered flight. The component of total reaction in the plane of rotation **opposes** rotation and is continually trying to slow the blade down.

At section B no part of the total reaction is acting in the plane of rotation — it is all rotor thrust.

At section C the component of total reaction is in the plane of rotation and **assists** rotation. It is continually trying to accelerate the rotor blade. Under these conditions it is no longer referred to as rotor drag, but is known as the **Autorotative Force**.

If we now consider the rotor blade as a whole, the section producing an autorotative force will be accelerating the blade whilst the section producing rotor drag will be trying to slow it down. To maintain a constant rotor rpm the autorotative section must be capable of balancing rotor drag section of the blade plus any ancillary drag (drive shafts, tail rotor, etc).

Under normal conditions, with the collective lever fully lowered, the autorotative rpm should remain in the correct operating band providing an adequate rate of descent exists.

If the collective lever is raised during autorotation the pitch angles will increase on all sections of the rotor blade causing the autorotative section to move outwards. At the same time, section D at the root becomes stalled and the extra drag generated causes a reduction in the size of the autorotative section and a rpm decrease.

Autorotation from high altitudes and/or high all-up weights mean higher rates of descent. Inflow angles will be higher and the autorotative sections further outboard along the blades, therefore rpm will be higher.

AUTOROTATION IN FORWARD FLIGHT

The autorotative force in forward flight is produced in exactly the same way as when the helicopter is in a vertical descent in still air. However, because of the changing inflow angle which occurs across the disc in forward flight, the autorotative section for the disc as a whole will move towards the retreating side where the angle of attack is greater.

If the engine fails during a hover in still air and the pilot lowers the

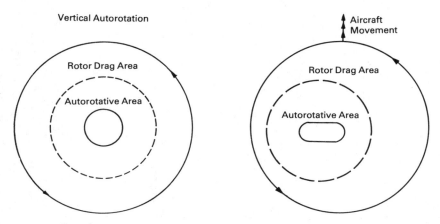

collective lever fully, the helicopter will accelerate downwards until such time as the angle of attack is producing a total reaction to give an autorotative force to maintain rotor rpm and a rotor thrust to equal weight. When this condition has been established the acceleration will stop and the helicopter will continue downwards at a steady rate of descent. If some outside influence causes the angle of attack to increase then there will be an automatic reduction in the rate of descent.

Compared with a vertical autorotation in still air the rate of descent will initially decrease with forward speed but, beyond a certain speed the rate of descent will start to increase again. The reason for this variation of rate of descent with forward speed is the changing direction of the relative airflow.

In autorotation, components of rate of descent will be required to produce a rotor thrust equal to the weight, a thrust component equal to parasite drag and an autorotative force to maintain rotor rpm.

If these components are plotted against forward speed a graph similar to the power required graph is produced.

Autorotating to give the maximum time in the air must be at the speed which gives minimum rate of descent. The speed for endurance will therefore correspond to the lowest part of the rate of descent curve.

Maximum range will be achieved when the helicopter is descending along its shallowest flight path, i.e. the best forward speed/rate of descent ratio. Relating this to the rate of descent curve, the optimum ratio will be at the speed where a line drawn from the

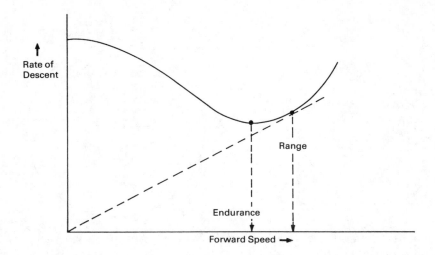

point of origin of the graph is tangential to the rate of descent curve.

When engine failure occurs in flight the helicopter has potential energy to dissipate. This is converted into kinetic energy during the autorotative descent.

The flare effect in autorotation will be exactly the same as for a flare in powered flight. Rotor rpm will increase because of the enlarged inflow angle which will cause the autorotative section to move towards the blade tip. The increased rotor thrust will reduce the rate of descent whilst the flare effects last.

When close to the ground the kinetic energy stored in the rotor system by virtue of its rpm is converted into work in the form of a large increase in rotor thrust by use of the collective lever. Thus the landing is cushioned but the rotor rpm decay rapidly as the kinetic energy is used.

FLYING FOR RANGE AND ENDURANCE

DEFINITIONS

Range can be defined as the **Distance** in air nautical miles that can be covered for a given quantity of fuel.

Endurance is the period of **Time** that an aircraft can remain airborne for a given quantity of fuel.

For both Range and Endurance the criterion is, of course, fuel consumption. The pilot must achieve the **minimum** fuel consumption in straight and level flight for Endurance flying and **maximum** efficiency for Range flying. In other words the best ratio of **Distance** covered to **Fuel consumed**.

ENDURANCE FLYING — PISTON ENGINED HELICOPTERS

In a piston engined helicopter fuel consumption is proportional to the power produced. Therefore the power required for level flight can also be said to represent the fuel consumption for the same conditions.

If we now consult the Power Required v Airspeed Graph it can be seen that minimum power is required at a particular airspeed if altitude and all-up weight are constant (point A).

It follows therefore, that at this speed there is minimum fuel consumption, thus satisfying Endurance requirements.

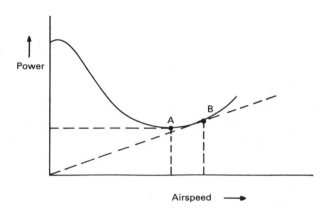

RANGE FLYING — PISTON ENGINED HELICOPTERS

Work is produced by fuel being consumed:

Fuel consumed = Work Done = Force x Distance
(the Force overcome aerodynamically is Drag)

Therefore **Work Done = Drag x Distance**

Now, $\textbf{Power} = \dfrac{\textbf{Work Done}}{\textbf{Time}} = \dfrac{\textbf{Drag x Distance}}{\textbf{Time}} = \textbf{Drag x Velocity}$

Referring back to the power graph, the vertical must then represent Drag x Velocity and the base line Velocity (True Airspeed).

If a line is drawn from the origin to the power curve, the lowest angle (point B) gives the airspeed for **minimum drag** and corresponds to the Range Speed.

TURBINE HELICOPTERS

The fuel consumption of a turbine engine is proportional to the **Thrust** being produced. At a steady speed Thrust equals Drag, therefore, if we consider the speed where there is minimum drag there must also be minimum thrust and hence minimum fuel consumption — this is known as **Endurance Speed**.

The turbine engined helicopter does not provide pure thrust but converts it into torque (shaft horse power) to drive the rotor shaft and is therefore similar to a compromise between piston and turbine engines.

Consequently the Endurance speed for a turbine helicopter is between the minimum power speed and the minimum drag speed.

To achieve maximum range with a turbine helicopter we must achieve maximum efficiency from both the engine and the airframe.

The airframe is most efficient at minimum drag speed.

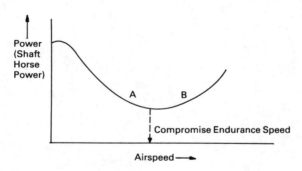

Engine efficiency improves with high engine rpm and achieves a lower specific fuel consumption usually at a speed greater than the minimum drag speed, therefore a compromise is necessary for maximum range.

The best compromise is to be found at the best TAS/DRAG ratio which occurs when a tangent is drawn to the drag curve.

ENGINE EFFICIENCY AT ALTITUDE

The supercharged piston engine improves with an increase in height until the throttle butterfly valve is fully open for a given boost setting (Full Throttle Height). Thereafter efficiency and power decrease.

The efficiency of the turbine engine improves as height increases because thermal efficiency improves (air is colder) and the compressor load decreases with decreasing air density. Thus engine rpm increase and specific fuel consumption improves.

WIND VELOCITY

Because of the relatively low speed range of the helicopter, wind can and does have a large effect on range flying. It can, in fact, be the main factor to consider when selecting the best height to fly at.

Flying at a higher altitude may give the advantage of a strong tailwind or conversely a strong headwind may mean flying low to improve groundspeed and distance.

WEIGHT AND BALANCE

DEFINITIONS

Basic Weight is the weight of the helicopter including basic equipment, oil, and unuseable fuel and to which it is only necessary to add the weights of Variable, Expendable and Payload items to arrive at the All-up Weight.

Basic Equipment is the non-expendable equipment which is common to all the roles for which the helicopter is designed. It includes unconsumable fluids, coolant, hydraulic and pneumatic systems.

Variable Load consists of those items which vary from flight to flight and which are not expendable in the air such as crew and role equipment.

Expendable Load includes fuel, oil, and freight which may be air dropped.

Payload is the total load of passengers and/or freight actually carried in the helicopter.

Maximum All-up Weight is the maximum weight at which the helicopter is permitted to fly.

BALANCE

Having determined that the helicopter will not exceed the limitations of all-up weight, the load must be correctly positioned to ensure that the centre of gravity remains within limits.

When hovering in still air conditions the attitude of the fuselage will vary with the position of the centre of gravity and it may be necessary to apply cyclic to keep the rotor disc level. Providing that the centre of gravity remains within laid down limits, cyclic stick will be adequate for forwards and rearwards flight.

The lateral centre of gravity position normally changes very little with internal or external loads. Any lateral displacement requires a compensating cyclic stick movement if the rotor disc is to remain level, therefore, to avoid running out of stick control, it is important not to exceed any lateral limitations (weight on winch, etc).

DETERMINING THE C of G

The centre of gravity position is determined by finding the moment of individual items of equipment about a given datum, adding together all the moments and then dividing the total moment by the total weight.

The turning moment is found by multiplying the weight of an object by its distance from the datum. Provided that all the moments are taken about the same datum it is immaterial where the datum lies.

It is important to note that with some helicopters there is a large change in the centre of gravity position as a result of using up fuel. Although the helicopter may be within the centre of gravity limits for take-off, it can go outside the limits during the flight.

STABILITY

When a helicopter is disturbed from its flight path and tries to return to that state without any input from the pilot, it is said to be **stable**.

Stability is best explained under two main headings.

STATIC STABILITY

If an object is disturbed and it then returns to its original position by its own accord, it is said to be **Statically Stable**.

If after being disturbed the object continues to move further away it is said to be **Statically Unstable**.

Should the object, after being disturbed, take up a new position different from the original it is then said to be **Statically Neutrally Stable**.

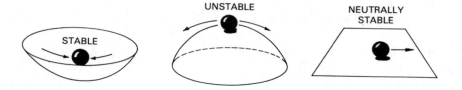

DYNAMIC STABILITY

If an object is **statically stable** it will return to its original position but, in so doing it may overshoot the position initially. If the amplitude of the oscillations die out it is said to be **Dynamically Stable**.

If the amplitude of the oscillations increase, then it is said to be **Dynamically Unstable**.

Should the oscillations continue but at a constant amplitude, it is said to be **Dynamically Neutrally Stable**.

STABILITY IN THE HOVER

Suppose a helicopter is hovering in still air when a gust of wind develops from the side. The rotor disc will flap away from the gust and if no corrective action is taken, the helicopter will move downwind.

After a short while the gust dies out, but because the helicopter is moving sideways it will now experience an airflow coming from the opposite direction. The rotor disc will now flap away from this new airflow and begin to slow the helicopter down. In addition, the fuselage will tend to 'follow through' and cause the disc to be tilted even further so that now the helicopter moves back towards its original position faster than when it moved away.

This movement of the helicopter will result in it experiencing continual sideways changes in airflow affecting the disc and, although it will be **Statically Stable** because the amplitude of the oscillations will be continually increasing, it will be **Dynamically Unstable**.

The same effect will be produced no matter what the direction of the gust is, therefore the helicopter is **Dynamically Unstable** in the pitching and rolling planes.

STABILITY IN FORWARD FLIGHT

If a gust of wind hits the rotor disc from ahead in forward flight it will cause the disc to tilt back thereby reducing forward thrust. The helicopter will now decelerate but as it does so the inertia of the fuselage will cause it to pitch up, tilting the disc even more to slow down the helicopter faster.

When the speed has stabilised the fuselage will then start to pitch down below its original postion because of a pendulum effect (pendulosity), whilst at the same time the rotor disc will flap forward relative to the fuselage (reduced flapback effect due to lower speed).

This now results in a speed increase with the helicopter in a shallow descent. As the speed increases the rotor disc will begin to experience flapback again and the whole cycle will be repeated but with increasing amplitude. If no cyclic stick correction is applied the helicopter could end up pitching outside its control limits.

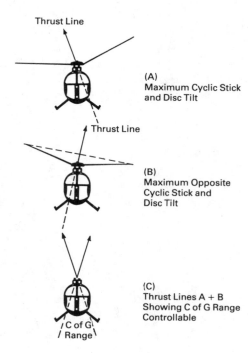

Thrust Line

(A)
Maximum Cyclic Stick
and Disc Tilt

Thrust Line

(B)
Maximum Opposite
Cyclic Stick and
Disc Tilt

(C)
Thrust Lines A + B
Showing C of G Range
Controllable

C of G
Range

The helicopter is therefore **Statically Stable** because each oscillation will take it through its original position, but is **Dynamically Unstable** because the amplitude of the oscillations progressively increases.

PENDULOSITY

The limit of control in a helicopter is determined by the amount by which it is possible to tilt the rotor disc, as this determines the tilt of the rotor thrust line.

For a condition of equilibrium to exist, the centre of gravity must align itself with the total rotor thrust line. The greater the distance between the main rotor head (centre of thrust line) and the position of centre of gravity, the more the attitude of the helicopter can change before reaching control limits.

STABILITY AIDS

One method of improving stability in forward flight is to fit a **Horizontal Stabiliser** at the rear of the fuselage. This will help in preventing the fuselage from 'following through' when a gust of wind causes flapback. As the fuselage begins to pitch up the increasing angle of attack on the stabiliser will damp down the movement thereby reducing the rearward tilt of the rotor disc.

The reverse takes place when the fuselage tilts down.

Adverse effects from the stabiliser can be produced when the helicopter is moving backwards. If a gust of wind causes the rotor disc to flap forward, the fuselage will slow down and the tail will pitch up, increasing the angle of attack on the stabiliser and causing the tail to pitch up even more.

CONTROL POWER

This can be defined as the effectiveness of the cyclic stick in achieving changes in fuselage attitude.

The main factor determining the degree of control power is the distance from the main rotor shaft at which a cyclic stick force is effective and this in turn is dependent on the type of rotor system employed.

Semi-rigid System

If a cyclic pitch change is made on a semi-rigid rotor head the rotor disc plane alters and the Total Rotor Thrust acting through the shaft is tilted. This then produces a moment about the centre of gravity position and an attitude change occurs.

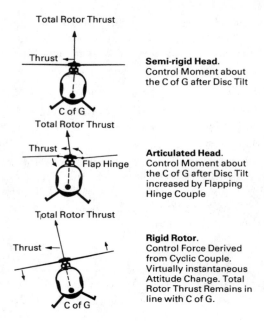

Fully Articulated System

As above, a cyclic pitch change alters the plane of the rotor disc and tilts the Total Rotor Thrust but the point at which cyclic force acts in effecting a fuselage attitude change is not only the shaft. The plus and minus application of cyclic pitch, as well as changing the rotor disc plane, is also felt at the flapping hinges. Thus a couple is formed which is additional to the single force of the Total Rotor Thrust in the semi-rigid head and therefore more effective.

The further the flapping hinges are from the centre of the head the greater is the effect of the couple in producing attitude changes with application of cyclic pitch.

Rigid System

A cyclic pitch change sets up an immediate aerodynamic couple to alter the fuselage attitude. The couple is estimated to be the equivalent of placing flapping hinges on an articulated rotor head at seventeen per cent rotor radius from the shaft.

If the same cyclic force was applied to the three rotor systems, the Rigid Rotor would be the most effective in changing the helicopter's attitude. The Articulated Rotor would be the next best and the Semi-rigid Rotor the least effective in terms of control power.

TYPICAL
EXAMINATION QUESTIONS

1. During steady forward flight the forces acting on the helicopter are:

   A) lift, equal and opposite to weight; horizontal thrust opposite to but greater than drag.

   B) lift, equal and opposite to weight; horizontal thrust, equal and opposite to drag.

   C) lift, opposite to but greater than weight; horizontal thrust, equal and opposite to drag.

2. Rise and fall of a main rotor blade from a mean position during rotor rotation is called:

   A) resonance

   B) flapping

   C) phase lead lag

3. The angle between the main rotor blade longitudinal axis and the tip path plane is the:

   A) coning angle

   B) angle of attack

   C) blade pitch angle

4. The main purpose of a clutch in a helicopter transmission system is to disconnect the drive to the main rotor:

   A) in the event of an autorotation becoming necessary

   B) to facilitate engine start up

   C) during engine overspeed condition

5. In order to increase total rotor thrust the helicopter pilot must:

   A) decrease the angle of attack of the rotor blades via the collective control.

   B) increase the angle of attack of the rotor blades via the cyclic control.

   C) increase the angle of attack of the rotor blades via the collective control.

6. The total rotor thrust derived from the main rotor is largely due to:

   A) the centrifugal effects of the rotating blades.

   B) aerofoil blade sections creating a low pressure region on their upper surface.

   C) aerofoil blade sections creating a high pressure region on their upper surface.

7. A 'vortex ring state' of the main rotor blades:

   A) is a vortex causing a stalled condition at the root end caused by high forward speed.

   B) refers to the tip vortices which occur in normal flight.

   C) causes an even higher rate of descent when descending with power on.

8. During one revolution of the main rotor, blade flap is the:

   A) rise and fall of the blade due to varying angular velocity.

   B) angular movement in the horizontal plane due to varying angular velocity.

   C) rise and fall of the blade due to varying aerodynamic lift.

9. The design maximum forward speed of a helicopter is either governed by the speed of the advancing blade approaching the speed of sound or by:

   A) the retreating blade approaching the stalled condition.

   B) the advancing blade approaching the stalled condition.

   C) the amount of collective pitch increase available.

10. One secondary effect which the tail rotor tends to produce if not corrected, is sideways drift:

    A) in the opposite direction to the tail rotor thrust, caused by the main rotor torque reaction.

    B) in the direction of the tail rotor thrust.

    C) in either direction depending on the amount of tail rotor thrust applied.

11. An increase in rotor rev/min causes:

    A) decreased centripetal acceleration.

B) increased centrifugal force.

C) increased coning angle.

12. When hovering near the ground:

A) lift is lost due to the increase in pressure under the rotor.

B) extra lift is obtained because of the increase in pressure under the rotor.

C) extra lift is obtained because of the decrease in pressure under the rotor.

13. Phase lag is the:

A) time between collective pitch increase and the restoration of the original rotor rev/min.

B) time between cyclic control inputs and rotor disc attitude change.

C) angle through which a blade moves between a pitch selection and the corresponding flapped position.

14. During autorotative descent main rotor rev/min is maintained by:

A) a lift force component created by the upflow of air.

B) form drag acting as torque after the reversal of airflow to upwards.

C) the inertia of the rotor head and blades.

15. Dynamic rollover may be caused by:

A) excessive yaw pedal movements to either the left or right.

B) an excessive rolling moment developing about a skid or wheel in contact with a slope or uneven ground.

C) excessive movement of the cyclic control in pitch only.

16. The purpose of fitting a horizontal tail surface to a helicopter is:

A) to counteract some of the nose down tendency in level flight.

B) the primary method of pitch attitude control.

C) to compensate for C of G movement in flight.

17. When rotating, the main rotor blade being of aerofoil section, derives lift:
    A) by producing a high pressure area above the blade.
    B) by producing a low pressure area above the blade.
    C) by acting like a screw on the air, allowing for slippage.

18. Stalling of a main rotor blade may occur on the:
    A) retreating blade at high forward airspeed.
    B) advancing blade at high forward airspeed.
    C) retreating blade at low forward airspeed.

19. The drag force of a rotor blade is opposed by:
    A) rotor rev/min.
    B) blade flapping.
    C) torque.

20. Changes in magnitude of total rotor thrust of the main rotor during cruise are achieved by:
    A) varying the speed of the main rotor, whilst the pitch of the blade is substantially constant.
    B) combined rotor speed change and blade pitch change.
    C) altering the pitch of the main rotor blades collectively whilst the rotor speed is kept substantially constant.

21. Ground resonance is:
    A) a standing wave vibration set up between the main rotor and the ground.
    B) a sympathetic vibration caused by main rotor and landing gear interaction.
    C) an effect which amplifies engine and/or tail rotor vibration on the ground.

22. The pitch angle of a main rotor blade at its most forward position is affected by:
    A) fore and aft cyclic stick movement.
    B) left and right cyclic stick movement.
    C) forward cyclic stick movement only.

23. Turning the helicopter in hovering flight may be achieved by the yaw pedals changing the:

    A) cyclic pitch of the tail rotor blades.

    B) speed of the tail rotor.

    C) collective pitch of the tail rotor blades.

24. When the collective pitch lever is raised the angle of attack:

    A) of all the main rotor blades is decreased equally.

    B) of all the main rotor blades is increased equally.

    C) of the blade in the forward position is increased and the angle of attack of the blade in the aft position is decreased.

25. Disc loading is defined as:

    A) increase in rotor thrust required to compensate for accelerations during manoeuvres.

    B) maximum centrifugal loading of the rotor hub assembly.

    C) the ratio of the total weight of the helicopter supported, per unit of the disc area.

ANSWERS

1.	B	10.	B	19.	C
2.	B	11.	B	20.	C
3.	A	12.	B	21.	B
4.	B	13.	C	22.	B
5.	C	14.	A	23.	C
6.	B	15.	B	24.	B
7.	C	16.	A	25.	C
8.	C	17.	B		
9.	A	18.	A		

2

HELICOPTER HANDLING

THE HEIGHT VELOCITY DIAGRAM

All helicopter manufacturers publish a height velocity diagram in the Flight Manual for their helicopters. The diagram depicts unsafe combinations of altitude and airspeed for each model type. Operating at altitudes and airspeeds within the shades areas of the diagram will not allow enough time to establish safe autorotation in the event of an engine failure.

ENSTROM 280

HEIGHT — VELOCITY DIAGRAM

For Operation at Sea Level (Tests conducted on prepared surfaces)

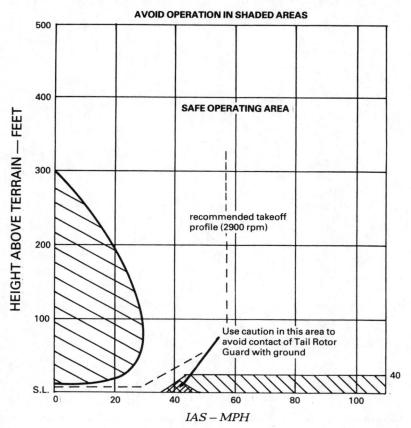

Since the diagram is plotted for flight at constant airspeed and altitude, an engine failure during climbout is more critical. During the climb the helicopter is operating at higher power settings and blade pitch angles. An engine failure at this time would cause rapid rotor RPM decay.

You should avoid low altitude and high airspeed conditions because your recognition of an engine failure will most likely coincide with, occur or shortly after, ground contact! Even if you do detect an engine failure there may not be sufficient time to rotate the helicopter from a nose low attitude to one that is suitable for slowing down and then landing.

Generally, if the helicopter is more than 500 feet above the ground you should have sufficient time to establish a steady autorotation. Between approximately twelve feet and 500 feet the ability to transition into autorotation depends on the actual height and airspeed at the time the engine fails. Below twelve feet you can make a safe autorotative landing by utilizing the inertia of the main rotor system.

It is important, therefore, that you should always be familiar with the height velocity diagram for the particular helicopter you are piloting.

PRE-FLIGHT INSPECTION AND ENGINE STARTING

Safe flying begins on the ground.

A pre-flight inspection is performed prior to each flight to ensure the helicopter is in a safe condition. The pilot in command is entirely responsible for making this decision.

Regardless of the number of times a procedure is repeated, a written check list should be followed step by step each time. Written check lists are used because of variations in types of helicopter and are recommended because they:

1. Provide an organized procedure for a complex operation.

2. Prevent duplication of effort whilst ensuring each item is checked.

3. Ensure that no important item is missed.

4. Help in making the transition to different models of helicopter.

5. Eliminate the possibility of forgetting items.

GENERAL SAFETY CONDITIONS

Helicopters are safe flying machines as long as they are operated within the parameters established by the manufacturer. There are, however, certain basic aspects of helicopter operation which require special considerations to ensure safe operation.

SAFETY PARAMETERS

Rotors and Immovable Objects

The exposed nature of the main and tail rotors deserve special caution. Care must be taken when hover taxying near hangars or obstructions since the distance between the rotor blade tips and the obstruction is very difficult to judge.

The tail rotor of many helicopters cannot be seen from the cabin, therefore, when hovering backwards or turning on a spot, plenty of room must be allowed for tail rotor clearance.

Rotors and People

People are fascinated by helicopters so caution must be used when operating near them. If people are to be allowed near a helicopter with blades turning then they should have been instructed in the safe techniques to use.

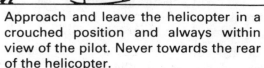

Approach and leave the helicopter in a crouched position and always within view of the pilot. Never towards the rear of the helicopter.

On uneven ground always approach and leave on the downhill side. Never on the uphill side.

A helicopter should always be approached or departed from the front. People approaching the helicopter with the blades turning should be instructed to stay low as they walk under the rotor blades. Because of wind gusts the rotors can flex low enough for the tips to hit a person of average height. They should also be instructed to hold on firmly to any hats or loose articles and never reach up or chase after an object that has blown away.

People should never be permitted to move aft of the cabin door and out of the pilot's view. Ducking under the tailboom should be absolutely forbidden due to the close proximity of the tail rotor.

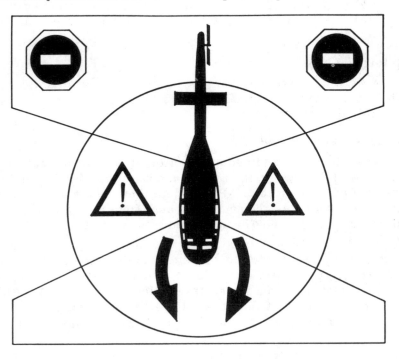

Consideration should also be given to the slope of the ground. Always approach up the slope and leave down the slope because the main rotor blade tips are closer to the ground on the upslope side.

Rotors and Debris

Another consideration is the downwash which the main rotor generates and which is capable of blowing sand, dust, snow, and water at high velocity for significant distances. This flying debris can cause injury to nearby people and damage to buildings and other aircraft. In addition, any airborne debris near the helicopter can be ingested into the engine intake or struck by the main and tail rotors.

Rotors and RPM

Rotor RPM is a very important aspect of helicopter performance. The normal operating range is limited to the green arc shown on the main rotor tachometer.

Minimum Rotor Speed

Several aspects of performance are incorporated into the minimum rotor speed. First of all, tail rotor speed is a function of main rotor speed. At low main rotor RPM the tail rotor may not be able to produce enough thrust to counteract main rotor torque. In this case directional control may be inadequate to prevent the helicopter from rotating to the right.

Rotor speed also relates to the thrust or lift produced. As the main rotor speed decreases, thrust is decreased by a factor of approximately two; that is, decrease in RPM of ten per cent results in a decrease in lift of almost twenty per cent. A main rotor speed below minimum limit will not produce enough thrust to sustain level flight.

One of the most important criteria associated with minimum rotor speed is autorotation performance. Helicopters must have the capability to autorotate to a safe landing in order to be certified. The minimum rotor RPM provides adequate controllability during an autorotative descent and landing. Below the minimum rotor RPM this capability is questionable.

Maximum Rotor Speed

The maximum rotor speed is a structural consideration. The blades, main rotor head and transmission have additional load factors incorporated into their design. The integrity of the rotor is protected by not exceeding the maximum rotor speed.

Airspeed Considerations

Helicopters are highly manoeuvrable flying machines. As such, they can be flown at three feet or three hundred feet above the ground at speeds ranging from a standstill to the maximum speed specified by the manufacturer. However, certain airspeed and altitude combinations must be avoided to provide favourable autorotation performance in the event of engine failure. Likewise, the maximum speed of a helicopter is limited by aerodynamic considerations. These performance aspects must be included in all helicopter operations.

STRAIGHT AND LEVEL FLIGHT

LEVEL FLIGHT

Flight training usually begins with instruction in the techniques of straight and level flight. The objectives being to point the helicopter in a particular direction, maintain the direction and fly at a predetermined altitude.

The pilot controls direction and altitude by controlling the pitch and bank with reference to the natural horizon – this is called **Attitude** flying. During training the pilot learns that there is a fixed attitude and a fixed bank, with respect to the natural horizon, for each flight condition.

The pilot must be aware of the differences between visual flying and instrument flying. Visual flying simply means that the natural horizon is used as the reference. Instrument flying is performed when the pilot refers to flight instruments for his attitude reference. This reference information can be derived from the attitude indicator, altimeter, directional gyro, magnetic compass and air-speed indicator. The emphasis during basic training will be placed on visual flying.

In straight and level cruising flight, the helicopter will be slightly nose down and laterally level in relation to the earth's surface. To maintain this configuration, it is necessary to establish the relationship of the helicopter to the natural horizon. One of the best ways a helicopter pilot can accomplish this is to use the distance between the horizon and the rotor tip-path plane as a reference. For any given airspeed, this distance will remain the same as long as the pilot sits in the same positioning the same type of helicopter. A straight and level attitude can then be maintained by keeping the rotor tip-path plane parallel to the horizon to control the bank

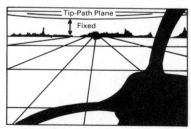

References for Level Flight.

attitude and a certain distance below or above the horizon (depending on the airspeed), to control pitch attitude.

In practicing straight and level flight the pilot learns to maintain a specific compass heading or a heading using outside references, and to establish the lateral and pitch attitude for level flight. He then periodically refers to the heading reference and altimeter to verify that he is on the desired heading and at the preselected altitude.

Attitude Flying

To attain the desired standard, the pilot must learn the techniques of scanning. He should develop the habit of keeping his eyes moving continuously between reference points as well as maintaining a watch for other aircraft. At no time should the pilot concentrate on any one reference.

Several forces may cause the helicopter to drift from the desired attitude. Power changes, turbulence and brief periods of inattention can all cause changes in heading or airspeed.

Since flying is a continuous series of small corrections, the pilot must learn to maintain the correct attitude as closely as possible and to make smooth, prompt corrections as necessary. Since the helicopter is highly manoeuvrable, abrupt changes can result in over-controlling.

The corrections should always be made in two steps. First the attitude deviation is stopped. If the heading or altitude is changing, control pressures are applied to return to the level flight attitude. Second, the attitude reference points are adjusted to make a slow correction back to the desired indication. After the corrections are made, the pilot should maintain the attitude reference to attain the desired flight condition.

Altitude and Collective Movements

The collective pitch control is the primary altitude control. Raising the collective increases the pitch of the rotor blades and through a cam linkage increases engine power. Both of these inputs cause the helicopter to gain height.

Throttle Control

The throttle is mounted on the end of the collective pitch control. It is used to control engine RPM. If the collective synchronization cam does not automatically maintain a constant RPM when the collective is moved, the throttle is used to adjust them. Rotating the throttle outwards increases RPM and inward rotation decreases RPM. Normally the pilot must co-ordinate throttle movement with collective movement. Both controls are sensitive, therefore control pressures must be used rather than control movements.

Directional Control and Cyclic Movement

The cyclic pitch control tilts the rotor tip path plane in the direction that horizontal movement is desired. In forward flight, moving the cyclic left or right will cause a roll (bank) in the respective direction. Moving the cyclic forward will cause the nose of the helicopter to drop and, likewise, a rearwards movement will cause the nose to rise.

Trim

Trim adjustments eliminate the need to hold continuous pressure on the cyclic to maintain a desired attitude. Trim is only used to relieve control pressure; it is not used to fly the helicopter. The proper procedure is to first establish the required attitude with the cyclic, then trim away any control pressure to maintain the attitude. Trim adjustments should be made whenever the pilot changes airspeed and/or power.

Effects of Pedal Movement

The anti-torque pedals are used to control movement around the vertical axis. As power is applied, the helicopter tends to rotate to the right due to torque reaction. Left pedal pressure is used as necessary to keep the helicopter heading in the desired direction. The opposite is true with a reduction in power – right pedal must be applied to maintain the heading.

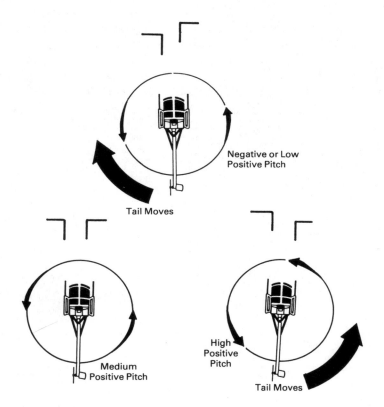

Pedal position in relation to tail rotor thrust.

Control Co-ordination

As previously stated, collective pitch control/throttle is primarily used to control power/RPM and altitude. The cyclic controls heading and bank and the anti-torque pedals control yaw.

In some phases of flight these controls have a secondary function. This secondary function may be so subtle and closely integrated with the primary function that the student pilot may have difficulty relating control movement to helicopter response.

As an example, consider maintaining straight and level flight at a constant power setting. To maintain the desired altitude the pilot should use cyclic pressure, as necessary, to maintain the desired attitude. Collective pitch is used to set and maintain the cruise power setting. Co-ordinated use of throttle is necessary to keep the RPM within limitations and pedal pressure to maintain balance.

Small altitude changes or corrections can be made with the cyclic. Larger changes call for co-ordination of collective and throttle and, therefore, pedal corrections. Airspeed changes are made by changing the attitude with the cyclic, adjusting the power with collective/throttle and maintaining balance with the pedals.

Any control input must be co-ordinated with any other control inputs. As the student gains experience this becomes second nature and he will be able to control the helicopter precisely and smoothly with seemingly little effort.

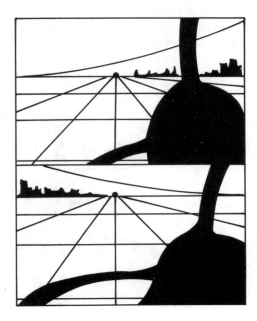

Attitude During Left and Right Turns.

To perform a climbing turn, the pilot should establish the climb as previously discussed. When attitude, climb power and pedal pressure are set, he should smoothly roll to the desired angle of bank.

The rate of climb is reduced during climbing turns because part of the rotor thrust is diverted to the turn, therefore, climbing turns are generally performed at shallow bank angles.

The desired heading and altitude are rarely reached at the same time. If the required heading is reached first, the turn is stopped and the climb maintained until the desired altitude. On the other hand, if the altitude is reached first then the nose is lowered to a level flight attitude and the turn continued until the desired heading. If both the required heading and altitude are reached at the same time, these procedures can be performed simultaneously.

Descending Turns

Descending turns to preselected headings and altitudes combine the procedures for straight descents with those used in turns.

The pilot should enter the descent in the manner previously described. When the descent attitude has been established, he should roll to the desired angle of bank. As with climbing turns, the initial procedure is performed in two steps. As the pilot gains proficiency, however, the descent attitude and bank are established together. As in any other manoeuvre, cyclic control pressures should be trimmed to maintain the selected attitude.

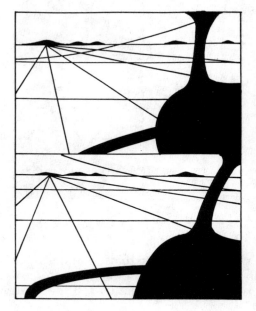

Left and Right Descending Turns.

When using visual references, the nose looks higher in a left turn than in a right turn although both are performed at the same airspeed.

Power is used to control the rate of descent. The pilot should make the initial descent power setting and allow the helicopter to settle in the descent. If a greater rate of descent is required, power should be reduced further. In contrast, power must be increased if the rate of descent is higher than desired.

The rate of descent is higher in a descending turn than in a straight descent with comparable power settings because the rotor thrust component is less when the helicopter banks. Compensation may be made with a slight addition of power.

After the ninety degree portion of the turn, pedal pressure is decreased somewhat to maintain the same rate of turn. Approaching the 180 degree position, opposite pedal pressure should be anticipated due to the tail moving from a position into wind to a downwind position. At this point the rate of turn will have a tendency to increase at a rapid rate due to weather-vaning. Because of the tailwind condition, the pilot will need to hold rearward cyclic pressure to keep the helicopter over the same ground position.

Maintaining the same rate of turn from the 180 degree position actually requires pedal pressure opposite to the direction of turn because of the tendency of the helicopter to weather-vane. If opposite pedal pressure is not applied, the helicopter will tend to turn at a faster rate into the wind. The amount of pedal pressure and cyclic movement throughout the turn depends on the strength of the wind.

Approaching into the wind heading, the pedal opposite to the direction of turn is used to stop the turn. Forward cyclic pressure is applied gradually to keep the helicopter from drifting rearward as a result of the headwind condition.

Control pressure and direction change continuously throughout the turn. The most dramatic change is the pedal pressure necessary to control the rate of turn as the helicopter turns through the downwind portion of the manoeuvre. Remember, left pedal requires more power, right pedal requires less power.

Turns can be made in either direction. In high wind conditions the tail rotor may not be able to produce enough thrust to control the rate of turn to the right. If control is ever questionable, a ninety degree turn should first be attempted to the left. If sufficient tail rotor thrust exists to turn the helicopter crosswind in a left turn, a right turn can be successfully accomplished. Normally, twenty knots of wind should be considered the maximum limit for crosswind or downwind hovering.

Hover Taxying

Hover taxying is used to move the helicopter at hover height. Two reference points in line and at some distance in front of the helicopter are used to maintain a straight ground track.

Forward movement is initiated with a small amount of forward cyclic pressure. As the helicopter begins to move, some forward cyclic pressure is relaxed to keep the ground speed low. Ground speed is controlled by applying cyclic pressure and should be limited to a speed equivalent to a normal walking pace.

After the helicopter is moving forward, rearward cyclic pressure will slow the helicopter or stop it, depending on the amount and duration of the control input.

Remember, cyclic controls ground speed, pedals control heading and collective/throttle maintain height/RPM.

Sideways Flying

Sideways flight usually starts from a steady hover and should be performed at a constant height and ground speed. The heading should also remain constant.

Sideward cyclic pressure in the desired direction will cause the helicopter to begin moving. Speed should be equivalent to a normal walking pace or less and is regulated by cyclic pressure. Forward or rearward cyclic pressure controls the helicopter's ground track as it moves sideward. Heading is controlled with pedals and height/RPM with collective/throttle co-ordination.

Backwards Flying

Backwards flying requires the flight path area to be checked before commencing the exercise.

Reference points are chosen in front of the helicopter to maintain a straight rearward ground track. Maximum hovering speed should be normal walking speed. Rearward movement is begun by rearward cyclic pressure. As movement occurs, rearward pressure is relaxed somewhat to maintain a slow ground speed. To stop the helicopter, forward cyclic pressure is applied and then released as movement ceases.

A straight ground track is maintained with lateral cyclic pressure whilst heading is held constant with pedals and height/RPM with co-ordinated use of collective/throttle. Hovering flight should be smooth and continuous without the helicopter yawing or changing height. This condition is achieved by using control pressures rather than control movements and by making small corrections immediately rather than waiting until the situation requires larger control inputs.

Recovery from Low Rotor RPM

A low rotor RPM condition is the result of the main rotor blades, having an angle of attack (induced by collective pitch), which has created so much drag that engine power is not sufficient to maintain normal operating RPM. If RPM are not regained soon enough, lifting power of the main rotor blades will be lost.

As soon as a low RPM condition is detected, additional throttle should be applied immediately and held whilst collective is lowered slightly to reduce pitch and drag. As the helicopter starts to sink, the collective is raised slightly to stop it. At hover height this technique may have to be repeated several times to regain normal operating RPM.

However, when operating at altitude the collective may have to be lowered only once to regain normal RPM.

Since the tail rotor is geared to the main rotor, low main rotor RPM will not allow the rail rotor to produce enough thrust to maintain directional control.

Hover Training Squares

Training squares are used to gain proficiency in controlling the helicopter in the hover. These exercises emphasize co-ordination of flight controls as specific ground tracks are followed.

Constant Heading Square

This pattern is started by hovering over one corner of the training square with the helicopter facing into wind. The helicopter is then hovered along one side of the square maintaining its into wind heading.

At each corner of the square, the helicopter is stopped before proceeding along the next side. The helicopter should move slowly and steadily along each side and the heading and height remain constant throughout the pattern.

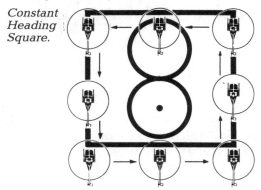

Constant Heading Square.

Parallel Heading Square

The parallel heading square incorporates downwind and crosswind hovering into the pattern. Therefore, this exercise should not be flown if the wind velocity exceeds the helicopter's limitations.

The pattern is started from any corner of the square. The helicopter is then hovered over the ground track with its longitudinal axis aligned with one of the sides of the square. As each corner is reached, the helicopter should be stopped before it is turned and aligned with the next side.

When hovering on the crosswind legs of the pattern, the cyclic is held into the wind to maintain the ground track. This cyclic input is co-ordinated with the pedal opposite the wind direction to keep the heading aligned with the ground track. At the same time, the collective and throttle are used to maintain height and RPM.

Downwind hovering requires continuous use of pedal pressure to maintain directional control. Changing pedal pressure necessitates co-ordinated throttle changes to maintain the proper RPM. Ground speed is controlled with cyclic.

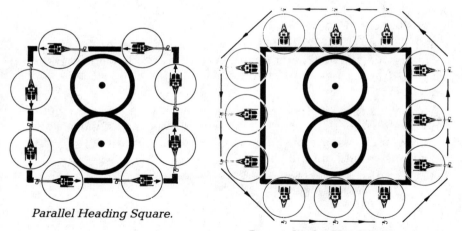

Parallel Heading Square.

Perpendicular Heading Square.

Perpendicular Heading Square

This exercise is flown with the helicopter outside the pattern with its longitudinal axis perpendicular to a side. The helicopter should not be stopped at the corners but turned in one continuous motion, using co-ordinated cyclic and pedal pressure, to align it with the next leg.

AIRPORT AND HELIPORT OPERATIONS

In today's flight environment, the responsibility for collision avoidance rests entirely with the pilot. Although several systems have been designed as safety aids, nothing can replace pilot vigilance.

Airport operations require constant effort on the part of the pilot to see and avoid other aircraft. The pilot should make a point of checking both the approach and departure path prior to take-off or landing. The use of landing lights will often make the helicopter more visible in times of reduced visibility.

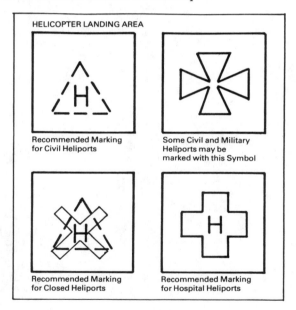

Helicopter Landing Areas.

During all operations, the pilot must maintain an awareness of blind spots which are inherent in the design of a given aircraft. Clearing turns should be employed to expose the airspace which has been hidden by components of the aircraft. Traditionally, helicopters have been designed with extremely good visibility as a result of large clear areas in the canopy. On the other hand, many light aeroplanes have large areas blocked by the nose and wing areas.

To see something clearly under normal illumination, an individual must look directly at the object. Experiments have shown that the eye perceives poorly if an image is moving across the retina of the eye. Therefore, when scanning for other aircraft, the scan should be carried out in sectors rather than permitting the eyes to sweep across the sky. Each successive sector of the sky should be brought into focus separately to provide the sharpest images for the eye to discern. Visual scanning involves the systematic search of the entire visual field through use of both eye and head movements.

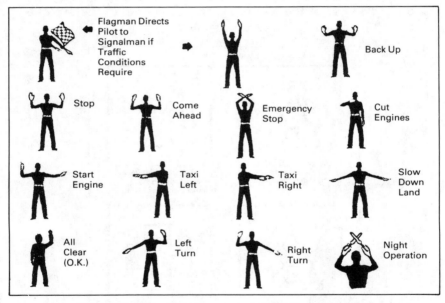

These are some of the more common hand signals.

TRANSITIONS

HOVER TO FORWARD FLIGHT

When the helicopter is hovering in still air, the total rotor thrust is equal to the weight. To achieve forward flight the rotor disc has to be tilted forward and the total rotor thrust must now provide both a vertical force to balance weight and a horizontal force in the direction the helicopter is moving.

This change of state from a hover to a movement in a horizontal direction is known as **Transition**. (Also from a horizontal movement back to a hover.)

When the helicopter is travelling forward at a uniform speed, the horizontal component, thrust, will be balanced by parasite drag. Since parasite drag increases as the square of the airspeed, the faster the helicopter is moving forward the greater must become the tilt of the disc to provide the thrust. But for level flight the vertical component of total rotor thrust must remain equal to weight. It follows therefore, that when the helicopter moves forward from the hover the total rotor thrust must increase.

As total rotor thrust is a function of collective pitch it would appear that the lever must be progressively raised for any given increase in forward speed. However, in practice it is found that for speeds up to 45–55 knots, depending on the type of helicopter, both the collective lever and power can be progressively reduced and it is only for speeds above this that pitch and power have to be increased.

This gain in rotor efficiency when moving forward is known as **Translational Lift**. The same effect will occur if the helicopter is hovering in wind conditions.

TRANSLATIONAL LIFT

When the helicopter has established a steady hover in still air conditions a certain value of collective pitch, say eight degrees, will be required to maintain the hover.

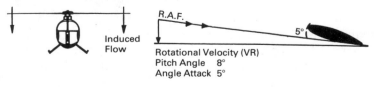

Induced Flow

R.A.F.

5°

Rotational Velocity (VR)
Pitch Angle   8°
Angle Attack   5°

It will be noted that the angle of attack, say five degrees, is less than the pitch angle. The angle of attack depending on the induced flow — if there were no induced flow the angle of attack would be the same as the pitch angle.

Consider now the effect of a twenty knot wind and assume that it is possible to maintain the hover without tilting the rotor disc. The column of air which was flowing **down** towards the disc will now be replaced by a mass of air which is moving horizontally **across** the disc. The rotors will act on this to produce an induced flow but with a reduced velocity.

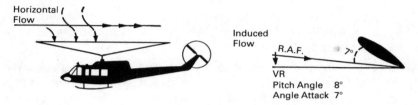

If the horizontal airflow is considered to remain parallel to the plane of rotation, then no part of it will actually pass through the disc.

However, to maintain the hover condition when facing into wind the disc must be tilted forward. The horizontal flow of air will not now be parallel to the disc and a component of it can be considered to be actually passing through the disc, effectively increasing the induced flow. To consider an extreme case, if the rotor disc was tilted ninety degrees to this horizontal flow then all of it would be passing through the disc at right angles to the plane of rotation.

The effect of this horizontal airflow across the disc when hovering into wind is therefore to reduce the induced flow, but because the disc is tilted forward a component of this horizontal flow will now be passing through the disc, effectively increasing the induced flow.

Providing the reduction in induced flow is greater than the component of horizontal airflow passing through the disc, then the angle of attack will increase. Therefore, the collective pitch can be

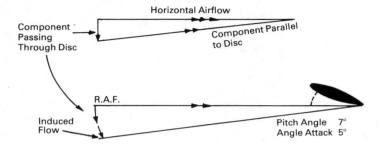

decreased whilst maintaining the same angle of attack.

The reduction of induced flow, **Translational Lift**, first takes effect when air moves towards the disc at about twelve knots. The reduction is appreciable at first but when the flow of air through the disc begins to increase again, collective pitch and power must be increased if the required angle of attack is to be maintained.

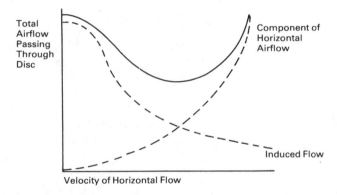

FORWARD FLIGHT TO HOVER

If the transition from forward flight to the hover is made by reducing the forward speed in stages and allowing the helicopter to settle at each speed reduction, then collective pitch and power changes would be the same but in the reverse sense as making a transition from the hover to forward flight.

However, the general method of coming to a hover from foward flight is by the pilot making a **Flare**. When this method of reducing speed is employed, collective pitch and power changes will differ considerably.

FLARE EFFECTS

To execute a flare the cyclic stick is moved back in the opposite direction to which the helicopter is moving. The flare will bring about a number of effects:

a) **Thrust Reversal**. By tilting the disc away from the direction in which the helicopter is travelling, the thrust component of total rotor thrust will now act in the same direction as the fuselage parasite drag, causing the helicopter to slow down rapidly.

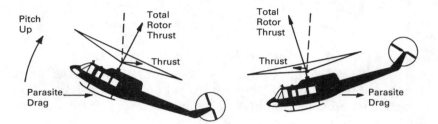

The fuselage will respond to this rapid deceleration by pitching up. If the pilot takes no corrective action the disc will be tilted back further still causing an even greater deceleration.

b) **Increase in Total Rotor Thrust**. Another effect of tilting the disc whilst the helicopter is moving forward is to change the airflow relative to the disc. As explained in Translational Lift, a component of the horizontal airflow due to the helicopter moving forward is passing through the disc at right angles to the plane of rotation in the **same** direction as the induced flow.

When the disc is flared, a component of the horizontal airflow will now be **opposing** the induced flow. The change in direction of the airflow relative to the blade will cause an increase in angle of attack and therefore an increase in total rotor thrust.

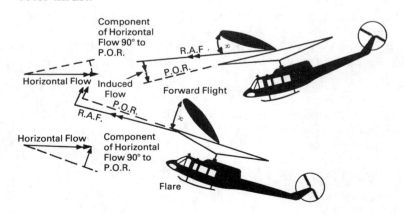

If no corrective action is taken the helicopter will climb, therefore, if a constant height is to be maintained the collective lever must be lowered.

c) **Increase in Rotor RPM**. Unless power is reduced when the lever is lowered to maintain height, the rotor rpm will obviously increase. They will also increase rapidly in the flare for two other reasons:

  i) **Conservation of Angular Momentum**
     The increase in total rotor thrust will cause the blades to cone up. The radius of the blades' C of G from the axis of rotation decreases and the blades' rotational velocity increases, therefore power must be reduced to maintain constant rpm.

  ii) **Reduction in Rotor Drag**
     Rotor drag is reduced in the flare because the total reaction moves towards the axis of rotation as a result of the changed direction of the relative airflow.

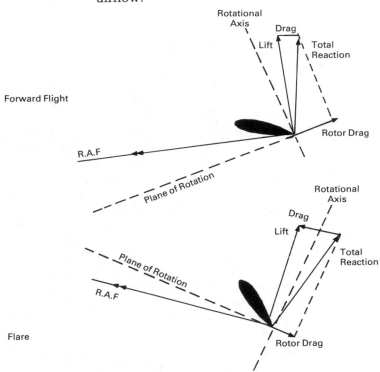

As engine power is being used to match rotor drag for a given rotor rpm, if the drag decreases then the power must decrease to maintain the same rotor rpm.

As a result of the flare the forward speed reduces rapidly and flare effects disappear. Collective pitch and power which had been reduced in the flare must now be replaced and, in addition, **more** collective pitch and power must be used to replace loss of translational lift caused by speed reduction, otherwise the helicopter would sink.

The cyclic stick must also be moved forward to level the helicopter and prevent it from moving backwards.

The power changes necessary during the flare affects the helicopter in the yawing plane, therefore pedals must be used to maintain the heading throughout.

A transition from the hover to the climb is normally done into wind. However, obstacles and other considerations may at times, dictate that the transition from and to the hover is carried out crosswind.

NORMAL TRANSITION – HOVER TO CLIMB

This exercise is started with the helicopter hovering into wind and transitioning into the climb over a predetermined ground track. During the transition a profile should be flown which avoids the shaded areas of the height/velocity diagram.

Prior to starting the transition, the pilot should carry out a performance check which includes power, balance and flight controls. The power check evaluates the amount of excess power available for the transition; that is, the difference between the power being used to hover and the maximum power available under the existing conditions. The balance of the helicopter is indicated by the position of the cyclic when maintaining a stationary hover. A wind will necessitate some cyclic deflection but there should not be an extreme deviation from neutral. Flight controls should move freely and the helicopter respond normally. These checks are usually performed as the pilot turns the helicopter to clear the area prior to transitioning. If any of these or other circumstances make the manoeuvre doubtful, a transition should not be attempted.

The helicopter is now started forward with a small amount of cyclic pressure. As the horizontal movement begins the helicopter will

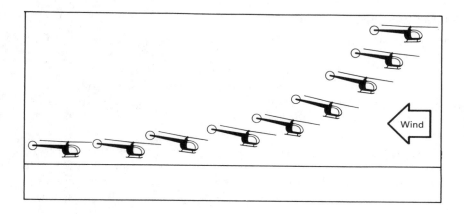

lose some ground effect and tend to sink unless power is increased slightly. Pedal pressure is used to control the heading.

As the helicopter continues to accelerate the advancing main rotor blade produces more lift than the retreating blade which causes the nose to pitch up (FLAPBACK). Forward cyclic pressure is used to compensate for this pitching moment. Power is used to maintain height and pedals continue to hold the heading. Further acceleration increases the mass airflow across the rotor disc causing an increase in rotor thrust (TRANSLATIONAL LIFT), and the helicopter rises. Cyclic pressure is used to compensate and establish the climb attitude and at the same time power is increased. This pitch attitude and climb power setting should result in a profile in which height and airspeed increase simultaneously.

Some important aspects of a normal transition are:

1. The extra power required because of the sink associated with reduced ground effect.

2. The bonus in lift acquired with forward movement – (Translational Lift).

3. Maintaining a straight ground track.

4. Holding a constant RPM.

5. Avoiding flight into the shaded areas of the Height/Velocity diagram.

CROSSWIND TRANSITIONS

Sometimes a transition cannot be made into wind because of obstacles, unfavourable terrain or other reasons. In a crosswind hover the cyclic is held into wind to prevent the helicopter drifting and opposite pedal is applied to keep it from turning into the wind. These control inputs are held, as necessary, through the initial stages of the crosswind transition and up to a height of approximately fifty feet.

After that the helicopter can be turned towards the wind by relaxing pedal pressure whilst maintaining the same ground track with the cyclic. (The technique of maintaining a straight ground track by turning the nose of the helicopter towards the wind is called 'crabbing'.)

APPROACHES

An approach is the transition from circuit height to either a hover or to the ground. Normally, it is a powered descent to the hover. The approach should terminate with the rate of descent and ground speed reaching zero at the same time. Approaches are categorized according to the angle of descent – normal, steep or shallow. There is no one correct angle of approach for the helicopter – the pilot should select the best one for the existing conditions. NEVER MAKE THE ANGLE STEEPER THAN NECESSARY. Regardless of the type of approach carried out, it should always be made to a specific landing spot.

NORMAL APPROACH

A well executed normal approach requires the use of techniques that consistently result in arriving over the landing spot without violating good safety practices. This requires a high degree of planning which begins on the downwind leg of the circuit. Several factors will influence the flight path along the approach.

Wind velocity and airspeed determine how quickly the helicopter flies the approach whilst power and ground speed influence the rate and angle of descent.

If the pilot uses different turning points or airspeeds on final approach each time then he will also have new problems to solve and his chances of terminating each approach consistently over the spot are greatly reduced. To preclude this situation the aim is to eliminate as many of the variables as possible.

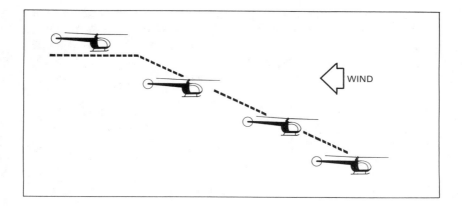

An attempt should be made to fly a consistent circuit pattern every time so that height, turning points, point of power reduction on final approach and final approach speed are the same each time.

CROSSWIND APPROACH

Basically, a crosswind approach applies the same drift control techniques as the crosswind take-off procedure. The turn on to final approach should be completed on an extension of the centreline to the landing spot and with the helicopter 'crabbed'.

On short final (approximately the last fifty feet), cyclic pressure is applied towards the wind and opposite pedal pressure is used to keep the helicopter pointed straight towards the landing spot. When the slip is performed properly, the helicopter has no tendency to drift from one side of the desired ground track to the other. These control pressures are adjusted, as necessary, during the transition to the hover.

GO-AROUND

A general rule of thumb used during the approach is to make a go-around if the helicopter is in a position from which it is not safe to continue the approach. Anytime the pilot feels an approach is uncomfortable, incorrect or potentially dangerous, the approach should be abandoned.

The decision to make a go-around should be positive and initiated before a critical situation develops. When the decision is made, it should be carried out without hesitation.

In most cases the go-around is initiated from a low power setting, therefore the first response is to increase power to the climb setting. Once the power is set, the cyclic is then used to adjust the attitude for the climb airspeed.

EMERGENCY PROCEDURES

Since a system failure in modern helicopters is very rare, most helicopter operations are conducted without any problems. There may come a time, however, when a malfunction occurs which, unless it is corrected or the proper procedures are followed, could lead to serious consequences.

AUTOROTATIONS

The most common reason for an autorotation is an engine failure which is indicated by one or all of the following: a sudden yaw to the left; decrease of engine and rotor RPM; absence of engine noise and loss of height.

Autorotation is made possible because of the Freewheel unit which allows the rotor system to disconnect itself from the engine drive system when engine RPM is less than rotor RPM. This allows the main rotors to continue turning. As the helicopter descends, upward airflow through the rotor disc drives the main rotors and the main rotor gearbox, which, in turn drives the tail rotor. Thus the main rotor stores energy which, if used correctly, cushions the engine-off landing.

The actual rate of descent in autorotation depends mainly on airspeed. Autorotative descents can be near vertical at low airspeeds and cover only short horizontal distances, or an airspeed can be used which produces the minimum rate of descent or maximum horizontal distance. Other factors affecting autorotative descents are air density, gross weight and rotor RPM.

The autorotation is normally terminated with a flare to slow down the forward speed, reduce the rate of descent and allow a touchdown at low or zero ground speeds.

The technique used for autorotation depends on the height and speed of the helicopter at the time of entry. Obviously, when the autorotation begins from a climb or level flight, the degree of success is improved if it is initiated at an airspeed and height outside of the shaded areas of the height velocity diagram. The diagram is not as restrictive if the helicopter is already in a descent.

ENTERING AUTOROTATION

The pilot should begin an autorotation by fully lowering the collective pitch lever. This reduces the pitch and drag of the main rotor blades to maintain operating RPM. As the collective is lowered the helicopter should be held level with the cyclic and at the same time, right pedal applied to prevent yaw.

The factors which should be considered when selecting the landing site are, whether or not the landing area is within the gliding distance of the helicopter, wind direction and speed, surface conditions and obstructions around the landing site. It is sometimes better to land crosswind if the area is flat and smooth rather than trying to land into wind on a rough or sloping surface.

To arrive over the selected area you can vary the airspeed, manoeuvre the helicopter whilst maintaining the minimum rate of descent speed, or use a combination of both. It is wiser to select a suitable area nearly beneath the helicopter and manoeuvre into it rather than try to glide to a distant one and end up short.

An autorotation can be made at airspeeds ranging from zero up to maximum glide angle speed. If the pilot slows the airspeed down to zero, a nearly vertical descent at a high rate will result. At sixty mph the minimum rate of descent is obtained. If the airspeed is increased further the rate of descent will increase. Whenever possible, the pilot should use the minimum rate of descent airspeed in autorotation.

During the descent, turns are normally made using only the cyclic stick. On some helicopters, pedal pressure during the turn may cause the nose of the helicopter to pitch down due to loss of airspeed, especially when left pedal is used. Normally, enough right pedal pressure is applied to maintain balance as power is reduced and then held in that position during turns.

Throughout the descent the pilot should continue to monitor the rotor RPM to ensure they remain inside the normal operating band. Because of the higher aerodynamic loads imposed during turns, the pilot must be aware and expect an increase in rotor RPM. The amount of increase depends on how tight the turn is and the gross weight of the helicopter. If the rotor RPM increase the pilot should gently raise the collective lever slightly to keep them in the green band.

If the autorotation is started between seven feet and 450 feet above ground level (limits of height/velocity diagram), such as on climbout or approach to landing, there may not be sufficient time or height for extensive manoeuvring. Under these circumstances the helicopter is normally landed straight ahead. When autorotation

the collective lever to reduce the angle of attack, increasing rotor RPM, reducing forward speed and avoiding excessive manoeuvring.

GROUND RESONANCE

Ground resonance is a phenomenon usually associated with fully articulated rotor systems. This condition can cause a helicopter to self destruct and occurs when the helicopter is in contact or partial contact with the ground.

If the helicopter is allowed to touch down firmly on one side, the shock is transmitted to the main rotor system. This may cause a vibration to set up which, if sympathetic with any inherent vibration, could amplify and resonate the helicopter to destruction.

The corrective action if flying RPM are available is to increase power and lift the helicopter back into the hover. If flying RPM is not available, close throttle and switch off immediately.

Skid type landing gear is not as prone to ground resonance as wheel types or skids with dampers.

DYNAMIC ROLLOVER

Dynamic rollover is the tendency of a helicopter to roll around one of its skids. This usually occurs during slope operations but can happen on level ground.

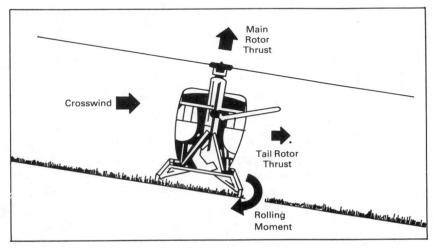

Factors Contributing to Dynamic Rollover.

There are several factors which can contribute to dynamic rollover. The main factor is the thrust of the main rotor when it is tilted downwind from the vertical. If the rotor system is not tilted or if there is no thrust, then dynamic rollover will not occur.

Other factors which contribute to dynamic rollover are the tail rotor thrust, especially when it is located high up on the helicopter, and a strong downslope crosswind. Also, in order for a rollover to occur, the skids must be in contact with a high friction surface. If the surface is slippery, the helicopter will tend to slide and not roll if a sideways force is applied. In addition, a helicopter with a high C or G and/or on narrow skid tracks is more susceptible to dynamic rollover than one with a low C of G and/or wide skids.

What makes dynamic rollover so dangerous is that the helicopter's C of G rolls around the skid; therefore, once a roll is started it may be difficult, if not impossible, to stop. Since a pilot may not be able to stop the roll, the only way to be sure a dynamic rollover does not occur is to be aware of the problem and try to eliminate as many of the contributing factors as possible.

PARTIAL POWER

Manifold pressure is a reliable indicator of engine performance. A loss of manifold pressure normally indicates a loss of power.

Partial power at altitude usually gives the pilot an opportunity to evaluate the cause and possibly rectify the problem. Turning on a fuel boost pump, verifying the fuel shut-off valve is fully on and making sure the magneto switch is at BOTH may help in restoring power. If it is not possible to restore normal power then a precautionary landing should be carried out.

If the situation develops whilst hovering, the pilot should land and report the problem to maintenance.

It is always wiser to make a precautionary landing than to compromise safety.

ALTERNATOR FAILURE

Malfunctions in the electrical power supply system can be detected by periodic monitoring of the ammeter. A broken or loose alternator belt or wiring is the most likely reason for alternator failure.

Problems of an electrical nature constitute an emergency and should be dealt with immediately. When evaluating electrical system malfunctions, the pilot should remember that the engine electrics are powered by magnetos and are not dependent on the aircraft electrical system or the battery, except for starting.

Electrical power malfunctions usually fall into two categories – excessive rates of charge or insufficient rates of charge.

After starting and heavy electrical usage, the battery condition may be low. This will cause it to accept a high charge rate during the initial part of the flight. However, after thirty minutes or so, the ammeter should be indicating less than two needles width of charging current. If the charging rate remains above this on a long flight, the battery will probably overheat and evaporate the electrolyte at an excessive rate.

Electronic components in the electrical system can be adversely affected by a higher than normal voltage. To prevent this possibility the alternator should be shut down. In this event, minimize the drain on the battery by turning the battery switch to OFF, since it can only supply the electrical system for a limited amount of time and terminate the flight as soon as practicable.

If the ammeter indicates a continuous discharge in flight, the system may be receiving insufficient power. If it shows a discharge with only essential equipment in use, alternator shutdown may be required. To check whether or not the system needs to be shut down, the pilot should watch the ammeter as the alternator is turned off. If the ammeter shows less discharge with the alternator off, the system should be left off.

If the alternator becomes inoperative, the battery will supply power to all electrical systems but only for a limited period of time.

If all the electrical power is lost or turned off, the pilot must realise how the remainder of the flight will be affected. Pitot/static instruments (altimeter and airspeed indicator), will continue to operate as will the magnetic compass. Communications and navigation equipment will not operate. All interior and exterior lighting will be inoperative. Rotor and engine tachometers will continue to function since they are driven mechanically. The manifold pressure will also work since it is pneumatically operated.

However, engine instruments which are electrically operated will not work, i.e. oil pressure, oil temperature, cylinder head temperature, fuel pressure and fuel quantity. The electric fuel boost pump will also cease to operate. Radio transmissions and the landing light should be used sparingly since they each draw electrical loads off the battery.

BATTERY

Insufficient battery power is generally caused by one of two problems – either the battery switch was left on after the helicopter was parked, or the battery or electrical system has malfunctioned. If the battery is low, the pilot should try to check to see if the battery has deteriorated, the battery switch was left on or if there is a malfunction in the system. The pilot should never count on a battery taking and holding a charge during the flight.

HIGH ENGINE TEMPERATURE

A high cylinder head temperature may be caused by a dirty or failed cooling fan, a broken shroud or merely hovering for a long time with high outside air temperatures. If the oil temperature is high, the oil cooler may be blocked or malfunctioning, the oil quantity may be low or of the wrong grade.

One solution may be to reduce the power setting to try to lower the temperature. If the temperature cannot be decreased to a normal value, a precautionary landing should be made at the nearest suitable place.

LOW ENGINE OIL PRESSURE

The engine needs a steady supply of oil in sufficient quantity and pressure for proper operation. For this reason, it is especially important to develop the habit of checking the engine instruments periodically, particularly during high power settings. A loss of oil pressure, for example, could easily go unnoticed until the engine overheats, runs rough or fails altogether. By the time these symptoms occur, it is already too late to prevent serious damage to the engine.

When low oil pressure accompanies engine overheating, the cause may be reduced thickness and pressure of the oil due to extra heat from the engine. When the oil pressure reading is low and engine temperature normal, a reduced power setting should be used until a landing can be made at a suitable place. If the situation is questionable, a precautionary landing should be made.

If a total loss of oil pressure precedes a rise in oil temperature, there is a good reason to suspect engine failure is imminent. In this case, an immediate landing should be carried out.

FIRES

Fires generally fit into one of three categories – fire during engine

WEIGHT AND BALANCE

The helicopter, like the fixed wing aircraft, has definite limitations of both all-up weight and balance. The total weight limits are set by the structural capabilities of the helicopter and allow for the extra forces encountered in turbulence and normal manoeuvres. Balance is perhaps more critical. Certainly the usual centre of gravity traverse for the single rotor helicopter is much less than the range of limitations for fixed wing aeroplanes. These limits are set by the range of movement of the cyclic pitch control system.

BALANCE

The method used for determining the balance point is identical to that used for all aircraft. To obtain the basic weight, the helicopter is depleted of all loose articles of the type which may be interchanged prior to any normal flight. In addition, such other variables as fuel are drained. The helicopter is then jacked up, supported at specified points, and the weight at each jack calculated. For ease, a reference datum is used, located at a point selected by the manufacturer, just ahead of the nose.

Every weight, or weight change, can be calculated as having a specific turning or lever effect behind this point. The basic C of G is calculated by finding the moments of the weight on each jack and then by taking these total moments and dividing them by the total weight. This basic C of G may well be out of the balance limits set for actual flight. It is the pilot's responsibility to ensure that, when everything and everybody is loaded, the C of G is then within limits.

To help in this respect, the basic weight and moment is recorded on a Weight and Balance Schedule. The pilot can then readily make a quick calculation to ensure safe flight when any unfamiliar balance condition is anticipated.

The practical balance limits are such that, in most helicopters, the C of G traverse will range from a little in front, to a little behind the point of suspension centred through the mast. This range will be predetermined by consideration of landing attitude, proximity of the tail boom to the disc and actual limits of cyclic control.

To permit the maximum of ease and safety, the engine mounts, fuel tanks and all other weight bearing points are located as close to the helicopter's point of suspension as possible. If they have to be positioned far from the centre, they are usually counter-balanced carefully by some opposing object.

Because the load is so frequently varied, the pilot has ample opportunity to become familiar with the weight and balance effects of any changes. A mental check of weight and balance should be included among the factors considered by the pilot in his pre-flight checks.

When in any doubt, the pilot should calculate the C of G as follows. The weight of each item added to the helicopter is multiplied by its distance from the datum; this gives its moment. All weights are added together including the basic weight of the helicopter. In addition, all moments are added together to give the total moment of the total weight. This total moment is then divided by the total weight to give the C of G. This can then be compared with the limits set by the manufacturer and the pilot can then readily ascertain whether he will be operating within those limits.

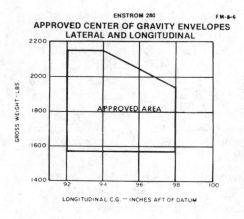

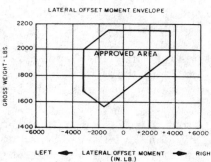

PRECISION TRANSITIONS

Helicopter manoeuvres are rarely rushed and, as a general policy, abrupt changes in attitude are avoided if they are not necessary.

There are circumstances, however, where a quick deceleration is imperative, for example, a helicopter operating in reduced visibility may have to stop suddenly to avoid obstructions. The manoeuvre required for this is a Quick Stop. Practising quick stops at low level provides an excellent means of learning advanced co-ordination.

Before such practice is attempted, Precision Transitions provide an intermediate training step. They require very little flare and as a result, deceleration is slower. The purpose of a transition is simply to move from one position to another at a constant height, heading and RPM. They are normally practiced into wind.

The pilot should avoid such manoeuvres facing downwind, especially if the wind is strong. The complete loss of translational lift whilst drifting downwind out of ground effect, could be quite dangerous.

The exercise is started with the helicopter being hovered into wind. The aim is to accelerate ahead to cruising speed and then decelerate back to the hover. This is an excellent co-ordination exercise. The helicopter is moved forward into translation with the cyclic. At first the helicopter will want to sink; this will call for an increase in power and pedal adjustment as necessary. As translation increases, the cyclic must be eased further forward to maintain acceleration and overcome flapback. The increase in translational lift will require a power reduction to prevent climbing resulting in a reduction of torque resulting in pedal adjustment as necessary.

After reaching cruising speed, the helicopter is then decelerated. The nose is raised gently to slow the helicopter down placing the rotor system in lightly flared attitude. This partial flare may create a slight increase of rotor thrust and, for a short while, it may be necessary to reduce power. Then, as translational lift fades away, the power is increased again.

The last part of the transition back into the hover is quite difficult to co-ordinate unless you take your time. The rotor disc has to be returned forward to the hover attitude at just the right speed to kill off the last bit of forward drift, without inducing the helicopter to back-up. This movement interferes with rotor thrust somewhat by removing any flare benefits just as translation is reaching a low ebb.

All of these effects put a heavy demand on collective and throttle and these must be applied smoothly to prevent sink. Up to now, the pedals have been subject to quite gentle adjustments to keep straight but this last power adjustment may call for a considerable application of left pedal pressure.

QUICK STOPS

Under normal operations, the quick stop manoeuvre can be used to slow the helicopter rapidly and return to the hover. It can be carried out at any height and airspeed; however, common sense dictates that the shaded area of the height/velocity diagram should be avoided.

During training, the quick stop is always finished heading into wind. It is usually carried out at around thirty to fifty feet above ground level at airspeeds of forty to sixty miles per hour. Here the manoeuvre is taught as a co-ordination exercise in maintaining constant heading, height and RPM throughout.

Normally, the quick stop exercise is begun from the hover although it can also be started from straight and level flight. A normal transition is initiated to a height of approximately forty feet and forty miles per hour. To commence a quick stop the helicopter is flared by rearwards pressure on the cyclic. To maintain a constant height, throttle/lever co-ordination is used to reduce power with pedal pressure to hold a steady heading. Exact and proper control pressures are required throughout the transition.

As the groundspeed decelerates towards zero, forward cyclic pressure should be used to lower the nose to a level attitude. Collective and throttle should be used as necessary to maintain height and RPM with pedals holding the heading. After the helicopter has stopped, gently reduce height to three to four feet above the ground.

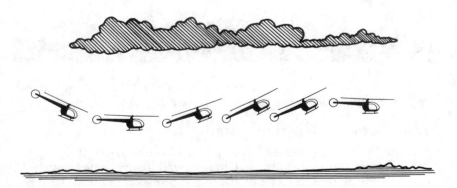

SLOPING GROUND

SLOPING GROUND LANDINGS

To land on a slope, the helicopter should be facing across the slope to provide normal ground clearance for the tail rotor. Whilst hovering over sloping ground, common sense should warn against turning the tail towards the slope.

From a steady hover, power is reduced in the normal way for landing. As the helicopter descends vertically the upslope skid will touch the ground first. From this point on, the cyclic must be held towards the slope. As power is further reduced, more cyclic pressure toward the slope is required to keep the rotor disc level and pedal pressure, as necessary, to maintain the heading. Any abnormal vibrations occurring as the cyclic is pressurized signals maximum cyclic deflection. In this situation the landing should be abandoned and the helicopter returned to the hover.

When the downslope skid makes ground contact, cyclic pressure is held towards the slope as power is reduced to a lever fully down position. During this phase the stability of the helicopter must be maintained to prevent the skids sliding down the slope. Once both skids are on the slope and the collective fully down, the cyclic and pedals can be smoothly centred. Flying RPM are maintained throughout.

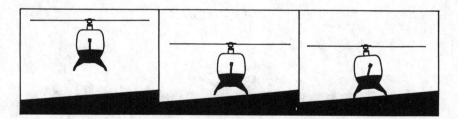

If at anytime the situation seems questionable, the helicopter should be lifted off to the hover and moved to another area.

TAKE-OFFS FROM SLOPING GROUND

A slope take-off is basically the reverse of the slope landing.
After setting flying RPM the cyclic is moved towards the slope until the rotor tip path plane is parallel to the horizon. This will hold the

upslope skid against the slope and allow a vertical lift-off rather than one perpendicular to the slope.

Holding the cyclic into the slope will cause the downslope skid to lift first when power is smoothly increased. As the skid comes up, cyclic should be moved towards neutral. If properly co-ordinated, the helicopter should attain a level attitude as the cyclic reaches the neutral position. Pedals maintain a constant heading throughout.

With the helicopter level and the cyclic centred, power is further increased to complete the lift-off.

RUNNING LANDINGS
AND TAKE-OFFS

Running landings and take-offs are most frequently used when insufficient power is available for normal techniques and where some suitable surface is available to provide the run-on into wind. Such a surface should be fairly smooth to avoid the risk of ground resonance during the prolonged period that the helicopter is running light on the skids.

For training purposes, the pilot should restrict himself to a power setting several inches below that required to hover. Calm, or light wind conditions, will offer the most opportunity for learning the use of limited power.

RUNNING TAKE-OFFS

The helicopter is positioned facing into wind with a clear area ahead. The left pedal should be adjusted to anticipate increased torque and the cyclic displaced slightly left to counter the tail rotor force introduced by the pedal. The cyclic is inclined sufficiently forward to start the run. If the skids are caught in depressions, twitching the tail with pedal adjustments will usually free one at a time and allow the helicopter to start moving. As speed increases, left pedal pressure is reduced to offset the increase of weather-cocking forces. The helicopter will become light on the skids and careful balance must be maintained. If the cyclic is held too far aft the helicopter will not accelerate. Throughout the ground run, the

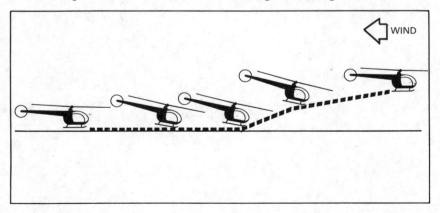

cyclic should be held sufficiently left to overcome the tail rotor drift effect. If handled correctly, the helicopter will gather sufficient speed to provide translational lift and rise slowly into the air.

RUNNING LANDINGS

After selecting a suitable landing run into wind the pilot should commence a shallow approach. The approach itself is very similar to that of a fixed wing aircraft. The round-out should be initiated gently at about forty feet above the ground and should be completed with the helicopter in the landing attitude by about ten feet.

The round-out is accomplished by a progressive backwards movement of the cyclic. After round-out, the cyclic should be adjusted to maintain the exact landing attitude, fore and aft as well as laterally. This attitude on most light helicopters is with the nose positioned just above the horizon. This attitude should prevent landing prematurely on the front of the skids. On the other hand, if the nose is too high, damage may be done to the tail rotor or boom as well as decelerating too rapidly for safe handling. The collective is used to control the sink as the speed reduces after round-out.

Throughout the landing run, sudden torque changes should be avoided or the helicopter may veer rapidly in response. The pilot should take care not to pull back too rapidly on the cyclic to slow down the helicopter, or the nose may rise suddenly and the tail rotor strike the ground. Also, quick aft cyclic movements whilst running over rough ground, may lower the rotor disc sufficiently to permit it to strike the fuselage with dire results.

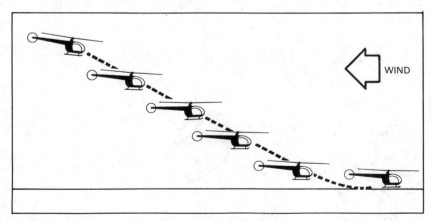

Run-on Landing.

TOWERING TAKE-OFFS
AND STEEP APPROACHES

TOWERING TAKE-OFFS

A towering type of take-off is used to depart from restricted areas and then climb over obstacles on the take-off path. Before attempting the take-off a power check should be carried out in order to determine the power margin available.

A towering take-off is begun from a low hover facing into wind. Power is increased to full power setting, pedals control heading and cyclic held to maintain a level attitude. As the helicopter ascends vertically the cyclic is pressurized forward to allow the airspeed to reach the best climb angle airspeed. (Normally around twenty-five to thirty mph).

When the obstacles have been cleared, the cyclic is then pressurized further forward and the attitude set for best rate of climb airspeed. Once this airspeed is reached, power can then be reduced to normal climb power.

As in any maximum performance manoeuvre, the pilot technique affects the results obtained. Smooth co-ordinated inputs coupled with precise control allow the helicopter to attain its maximum output.

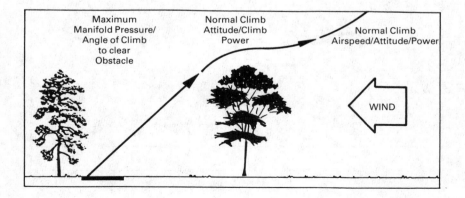

Maximum Manifold Pressure/ Angle of Climb to clear Obstacle

Normal Climb Attitude/Climb Power

Normal Climb Airspeed/Attitude/Power

WIND

STEEP APPROACHES

A steep approach is used for landing in a restricted or confined area.

Factors such as gross weight, density altitude and wind velocity have to be taken into consideration for each situation, therefore, a power check should always be carried out beforehand to determine excess power available.

A steep approach is usually begun at a slightly lower airspeed than normal (Enstrom/Hughes 300 – fifty to fifty-five mph), with power being reduced to initiate the descent. As in a normal approach, power is used to control the rate and angle of descent, cyclic to control groundspeed and pedals the heading.

Care must be exercised with steep approaches not to allow high rates of descent as these, coupled with low airspeed and power on, are conducive to vortex ring. (Settling with power.)

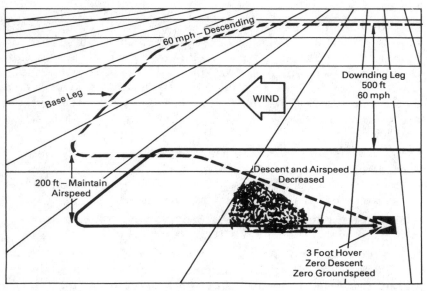

Steep Approach Profile.

CONFINED AREA PROCEDURES

A confined area is an area where the operation of the helicopter is limited by some type of obstruction – either natural or man-made.

Several areas of caution must be included in confined area operations. Adequate clearance must be maintained between the rotors and surrounding obstacles. The tail rotor deserves special consideration as it cannot be seen from the pilot's seat in most helicopters. Wires are especially difficult to see; however, the poles or towers supporting them are usually a good indication of their presence and height.

Wind and associated turbulence should be expected around obstacles. Updraughts on the windward side and downdraughts on the leeward side are normal and should be anticipated in winds of ten knots or more.

Forced landing areas should be included when planning the approach. The pilot should also leave himself a way out in case the landing cannot be completed and a go-around is necessary. A high reconnaissance flight over the confined area first will usually provide input for these contingencies. A height of some 300 to 500 feet above the landing area normally provides a suitable compromise between visibility and safety whilst flying over the obstacles.

Occasionally, a low reconnaissance may be necessary. The pilot should study his approach path and the immediate vicinity of his intended landing point. In addition, he should take advantage of the lowest obstacles and most favourable terrain.

The decision point must be established on the approach beyond which the pilot is committed to landing.

Throughout the approach, landing and departure, the helicopter should be operated as near normal as possible. On take-off for example, it is better to clear an obstacle by a reasonable margin with reserve power than to use maximum power to climb over the obstacle with wasted clearance.

Each situation requires an evaluation of pilot ability, helicopter performance, surface conditions and wind velocity so that flight techniques can be adapted to suit each case.

Whatever the technique, the pilot should utilize the advantages of ground effect, translational lift and wind whenever possible.

PINNACLE OPERATIONS

A pinnacle can be defined as a landing area from which the surrounding terrain is downwards in all directions. A rooftop helipad, for example, could be considered as a pinnacle operation.

Before beginning his approach the pilot should first fly over the landing area to collect as much information as possible about the site, wind, turbulence, forced landing areas and any other factors which could influence the approach and landing.

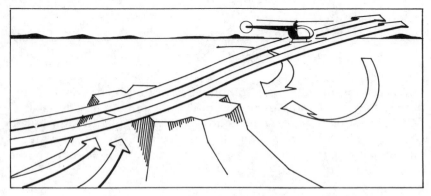

Pinnacle Downdraughts.

With this information, a decision can be made as regards the flight path and the type of approach to be flown. Whenever possible, a normal angle of approach should be used. (Never use a steeper angle than is necessary.)

When flying a shallow approach to a pinnacle, the pilot should avoid those areas where downdraughts are present, especially when power is limited. If downdraughts are encountered, the pilot may have to make an immediate turn away from the pinnacle to avoid being forced into the rising terrain.

During the approach, the pilot should be continuously verifying the information gained on the flyover earlier. As the approach progresses, the pilot must evaluate the feasibility of the landing and any changes to the plan should be made as they become necessary. If the situation becomes questionable, a go-around should be initiated immediately.

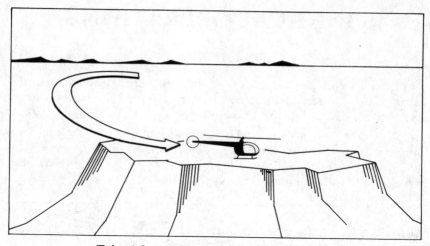

Take Advantage of Long Axis of Pinnacle.

Before taking-off, the pilot should carry out a power check in the normal way and evaluate the best route for climbout and departure. The pilot should plan the departure profile placing priority on gaining airspeed rather than altitude. This technique provides a more rapid departure from the area, an improved glide angle and a greater range in case of a forced landing.

NIGHT FLYING

In many respects, night flying is easier and more pleasant than daytime flying. Other aircraft are usually easier to see and the air is generally smoother resulting in a more comfortable flight. In addition, the night pilot experiences less traffic and often finds less competition when using the radio.

NIGHT FLYING CONSIDERATIONS

On a bright moonlit night when visibility is good and the air is calm, night flying is not a great deal different than flying by day. However, the pilot should consider the following factors carefully before making a night flight.

> Visibility
> Amount of outside light available
> General weather situation
> Proper functioning of the helicopter and its systems
> Night flying equipment
> The pilot's recent night flying experience

Pre-flight Inspection

The pre-flight inspection should preferably be carried out in a well lit area and with the aid of a torch. The canopy should be checked for cleanliness to avoid dirt interfering with the pilot's vision. Although this is a good pre-flight procedure anytime, it is especially important before a night flight.

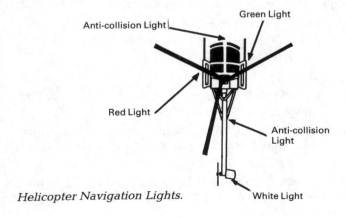

Helicopter Navigation Lights.

LIGHTS

Navigation Lights

All aircraft operating between sunset and sunrise are required by law to have operable navigation lights. These lights are turned on during the pre-flight inspection so they can be checked visually for proper operation.

At night, navigation lights should be on any time the engine is operating. A red navigation light is located on the left side of the helicopter, a white light on the tail and a green light on the right side.

Landing and Taxi Lights

Most helicopters have landing lights to illuminate the ground as needed when hover-taxying. The same light is used during take-off and landing at the pilot's discretion.

Although the landing light must be checked visually for correct operation during the pre-flight inspection, it should not be allowed to operate for any length of time with the engine shut down because of the high drain on the battery.

Care should be taken during the operation of landing/taxying lights to avoid shining them in the direction of other aircraft, since this can impair the other pilot's night vision.

Anti-collision Lights

All recently manufactured aircraft certified for night flying must incorporate anti-collision lights to make them more visible to other pilots at night.

The most common type is a rotating beacon which normally emits red flashes of light at a rate of approximately one flash per second.

An increasing number of aircraft are equipped with brilliant flashing red or white strobe lights which can be seen for many miles at night.

Instrument Panel Lights

All modern aircraft are equipped with some system for lighting the instruments and instrument panel.

Although a pre-flight functional test is carried out, a torch should always be carried on night flights to provide an emergency light source in case of failure of the interior lights.

Panel lighting is generally controlled by a rheostat switch which allows the pilot to select the lighting intensity which best satisfies his needs. The light intensity should be adjusted just bright enough so that the pilot is able to read the instruments. If the light is too bright, a glare will result and night vision suffers.

Normally one of three types of panel lighting is used:

Flood Lighting

Flood lighting is a common method of illuminating the entire instrument panel with one light source. With this system, a single roof mounted light is used with a rheostat to regulate the intensity. Its beam is directed both over the flight and engine instruments. Flood lighting seems to produce the most glare if the intensity is too high.

Post Lighting

When post lighting is installed, each instrument has its own light source adjacent to it. Each post light beam is directed at the instrument and is shaded from the pilot's eyes.

Internal Lighting

Internal instrument lighting is similar to post lighting except that the light source is located inside the instrument itself.

The magnetic compass and radios generally utilize internal lighting. Luminescent lettering is often used with internal lighting to permit instrument interpretation with less light. This type of lighting normally produces the least amount of glare and is found in many modern aircraft.

VISION

Night Vision

The ability to see at night can be greatly improved if the pilot understands and applies certain techniques. If the pilot's eyes are exposed to strong light, even briefly, night vision is temporarily destroyed. For this reason, avoidance of strong light must begin well in advance of a night flight.

It has been found that the adaptation required for night vision is decreased most quickly and completely by exposure to white light whilst red light has been found to be the least detrimental. Although red light is most desirable, its use results in the disturbance of normal colour relationships.

Off-centre Vision

Central vision is normally used to see objects. However, under low light conditions it becomes ineffective. For this reason the pilot should not look directly at objects at night. The object can usually be seen more clearly if the gaze is directed slightly above, below or to one side of the object. It has been found that looking about ten degrees off centre permits better viewing in low levels of lighting.

CABIN FAMILIARIZATION

One of the first steps in the preparation for night flying is becoming thoroughly familiar with the helicopter's cabin, instrumentation and control layout.

It is recommended that the pilot practice locating each control, instrument and switch, both with and without cabin lights. Since the markings on some switches and circuit breaker panels may be hard to read at night, the pilot must assure himself that he is able to locate and use these devices in poor lighting conditions.

AIRPORT LIGHTING

The painted markings on airports are not especially useful to pilots at night since they are difficult to see. Various types of lighting aids are used to mark and identify different sections of the airport for night operations.

Taxiways are marked along their edges with blue lights to distinguish them from runways which have white lights along their edges. The intensity of runway and taxi lights can be controlled from the control tower and may be adjusted at the request of the pilot. The threshold of a runway is marked with two or more green lights and obstructions or unusable areas are marked with red lights.

ENGINE START-UP AT NIGHT

Caution should be used with the engine start-up procedure at night since it is difficult for other people to determine the pilot's intentions. Turning on the navigation lights can help warn others that the engine is about to be started.

HOVER TAXYING AT NIGHT

Landing lights normally cast a beam that is narrow and concentrated. Because of this, illumination to the side is minimal and taxi speed should be slower than normal. Initially, judgement of distances is difficult and it takes some adaptation to taxi within the limitations of the area covered by the landing light.

TRANSITION FROM THE HOVER TO THE CLIMB

The contrast between day and night flight can be minimized by arranging a night checkout which begins at twilight. This will allow take-offs, landings and circuit work to begin in a more familiar environment. As darkness increases, the change to night conditions is made gradually. The pilot should select a point down the departure path for directional reference. During his first night take-off, the pilot may notice the lack of reliable outside visual references after he is airborne. Therefore a towering type of take-off should be used for all night departures.

During the climbout the pilot should continue to monitor attitude, airspeed and altimeter to verify the desired profile. The first 500 feet of height is considered to be the critical period in transitioning from a comparatively well lit area into what sometimes appears to be total darkness.

VISUAL IMPRESSIONS AT NIGHT

During the early stages of night training, most pilots find the initial visual impressions after departing the airport to be vastly different to those they are accustomed to during daytime flying. Therefore, orientation in the local flying area helps the pilot relate chart information to actual terrain and landmarks under night conditions.

The outlines of major cities and towns are clearly discernable at night and, under favourable conditions, are visible from great distances, depending on flight altitude.

On clear, moonlit nights, outlines of the terrain and other features are dimly visible. However, on dark nights, terrain features are nearly invisible except in brightly populated areas.

COLLISION AVOIDANCE AT NIGHT

The position of other aircraft at night can be determined by scanning for navigation lights and anti-collision beacons. Since the arrangement of red and green position lights is the same as that used on boats and ships, the 'Red right – returning' memory aid is applicable. In other words, if the pilot observes red and green navigation lights and the red light is positioned on the right, the other aircraft is approaching.

If the white position light is visible, the other aircraft is on a heading that will take it away from the pilot's immediate area.

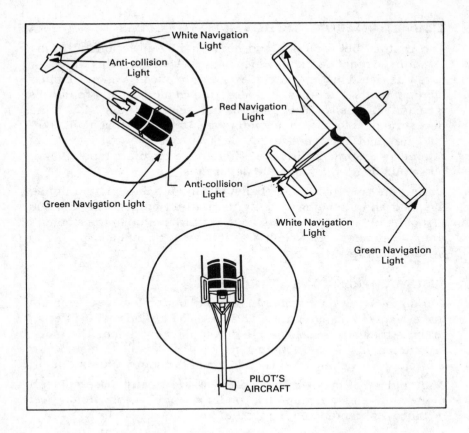

Position Lights and Direction of Flight.

WEATHER

The pilot operating at night must be especially attentive to signs of changing weather conditions. A pilot who is accustomed to daytime flying generally is not aware that it is extremely easy to fly into overcast at night because the clouds are not easily detected by visual observation.

A pilot approaching overcast can sometimes detect the presence of cloud because lights in the far distance will disappear. In addition, a luminous glow or halo around the navigation lights indicates imminent or actual penetration of cloud.

Before flying at night, the pilot must obtain a thorough weather briefing and pay attention to any indications of cloud formations, fog, icing and precipitation.

En-ROUTE PROCEDURES

In order to provide safety margins, the choice of high cruising altitudes is recommended. There are several reasons for this. First, range is usually greater at higher altitudes. Second, autorotative distance is greater in the event of engine failure. Third, pilotage and radio navigation are often less difficult.

A major consideration in planning a night flight is to ensure that enough fuel with adequate reserves is carried. A useful guideline is to reduce the daytime range of the helicopter by one third when flying at night. This has the advantage that the pilot is not tempted to stretch his range and the additional fuel can be useful to circumnavigate adverse weather.

Special attention should be given to the terrain elevations provided on the charts to ensure adequate obstruction clearance.

EMERGENCY LANDINGS

If a forced landing becomes necessary at night, the same procedures as recommended for daytime emergencies apply. If available, the landing light should be turned on to assist in avoiding obstacles in the final stages of the approach.

NIGHT APPROACHES AND LANDINGS

In some respects, night approaches and landings are actually easier than daytime ones since the air is generally smoother and the disrupting effects of turbulence and excessive crosswinds are usually absent. However, there are a few special considerations that apply to night approaches.

When landing at an airport at night – especially at an unfamiliar one – it is wise to make the approach to the lighted runway and then hover taxi using the lighted taxyways to the parking area. The heliport or runway lights provide an effective visual clue for judging the night approach. The lights seem to rise and spread laterally as the pilot nears the touchdown point.

Most pilots use the landing light for night landings, however, there is a point to be considered when it is used. The portion of the landing area illuminated by the landing light seems higher than the dark area surrounding it. This effect tends to cause the pilot to terminate his approach higher than normal. Also focusing attention on one point in front of the helicopter is poor practice. When using the landing light, the pilot's sighting point should be at least on the forward limit of the lighted area.

Proper training for night flying should include landings made both with and without the aid of the landing light. Proficiency in performing landings without the landing light requires practice but, after the first few approaches and touchdowns, they can be performed accurately.

PILOT NAVIGATION

Air navigation is the art of guiding an aircraft through the air so that it may arrive at a desired position, within the limits required by its operational role.

Pilot navigation is basically the same as conventional 'navigator' navigation, the difference being one of technique only. The limitations of cockpit space preventing the use of plotting instruments and the pre-occupation of the pilot with flying the aircraft, demanding a more simplified procedure.

Pilot Navigation Problems

For the Pilot Navigator, flying and navigation are allied activities. The predominance of one or of the other being decided by the operational role. The navigational factors contributing to a successful flight are

> The need for accurate flying.
> Pre-flight planning.
> Helicopter performance.
> Mental Dead Reckoning.
> Map analysis and Map Reading.

PRE-FLIGHT PLANNING

Accurate pre-flight planning, amended in flight as necessary by rapid mental calculations, will contribute materially to the success of any flight.

A pilot, by careful study of his route before take-off, can form a mental picture of his track which will greatly simplify the recognition of landmarks. By flight planning, he can confine map reading to definite times when check features are scheduled to appear. The sense of preparedness for what lies ahead has considerable influence on successful air navigation.

SURFACE W/V	MANCHESTER HELICOPTER CENTRE TELEPHONE: 061-787 7125	TRANSPONDER CODES	
		CONSPICUITY	4321
		EMERGENCY	7700
		RADIO FAILURE	7600

GROUND STATION .... THIS IS HELICOPTER ....

PRE FLIGHT RADIO CHECK AND AIRFIELD INFORMATION OVER

READABILITY .... RUNWAY ....RH LH

QFE .... QNH .... REGIONAL QNH ....

	T.A.S.	W		VAR. V				EMERGENCY 121.5		
STAGE	TRACK T	HDG T	HDG M	G.S.	DIST.	TIME	DEPART TIME	E.T.A.	A.T.A.
GROUND STATION CALLSIGN FREQUENCY									

.............................RADAR

THIS IS HELICOPTER ....
REQUEST M.A.T.Z. PENETRATION OVER

G .... IS A ....

POSITION ....

HDG ....

ALT ....

FROM ....

TO ....

.... THIS IS

HELICOPTER .... OVER

G .... IS A ....
VFR/STUDENT X/C

FROM ....

TO ....

POSITION ....

ALTITUDE ....

ESTIMATE ....

AT ....

REQUEST ....

JOINING INSTRUCTIONS

R/W .............................R.H. L.H.

QNH ....

QFE ....

F.R.E.D.A.	D/W CHECKS
FUEL	FUEL
RADIO	T/P's
ENGINE T/P's	HT/SPEED
DIRECTION GYRO	HEADING
ALTIMETER	LOOKOUT

Ideal Flight Procedure

For normal flights, pre-flight planning should be carried out on a basis which will require the pilot to map read at the following intervals:

Immediately after take-off to provide a definite point of departure and to establish a time of departure.

At points along the track to check the progress of the flight so that any deviations from the flight plan can be noted and modified.

At a final point to the destination so that previous alterations may be confirmed and final adjustments made as necessary.

Preparation of Maps

No hard and fast rules can be laid down for preparing maps. A track line is required to provide a datum for checking flight progress. Intervals along the track may be indicated by any of the following:

Time Scales: These can be at intervals of a suitable number of minutes at the estimated groundspeed.

Proportional Division: The track may be marked at quarter, half and threequarter distance intervals and annotated with corresponding flight times.

Distance Scales: Five mile intervals will provide a useful reference in estimating distances and in applying the 1:60 rule.

Dotted lines drawn at five degrees on either side of the track through departure and destination points are most useful for examination of heading alternatives.

The maps should be folded so that the complete track coverage is possible with the minimum number of page turns but without refolding in flight. They should be numbered and stacked in order of use for insertion in the cockpit.

MENTAL DEAD RECKONING

Mental DR is the mental calculation of the helicopter's progress so that its position can be assessed and adjusted, to arrive accurately at the required destination.

Drift lines are useful for the estimation of quick alterations of heading by locating the positions of pinpoints en-route with respect to the intended track and drift lines. When the track error is determined in relation to the point of departure, heading is altered by doubling the track error towards the intended track. Then an

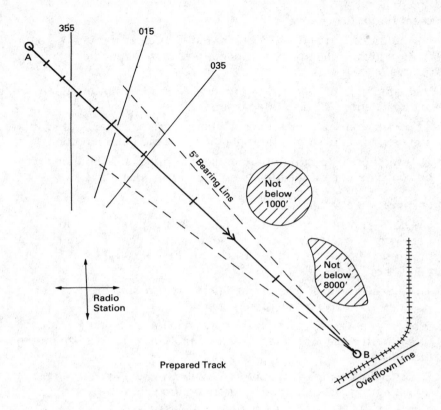

appropriate adjustment, equal to track error is made when the intended track has been regained. This technique is suitable for up to half way along track, beyond this point a closing angle should be estimated. (Closing angle is the angle between the new required track to the destination and the original track.) The required alteration for the destination is then the track error plus the closing angle.

The 1:60 Rule

The 1:60 rule is based upon the fact that one mile subtends an angle of one degree at an approximate distance of sixty miles. In applying the rule, the triangle relevent to the navigational problem is identified and the ratio of the length of the long side to sixty is established. This ratio may then be applied to the angle to reveal the length of the side opposite to it, or conversely, to the opposite side to reveal the angle it subtends.

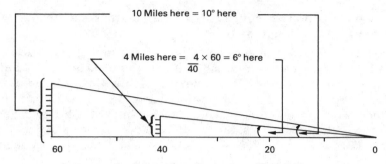

Basic Application of the One-in-Sixty Rule.

The assumption that a specific alteration of heading will result in a corresponding alteration in track is not strictly true because the direction relative to the wind is altered; consequently the drift may not remain as it was before. For alterations up to twenty degrees however, the change of drift can be neglected. For track alterations greater than twenty degrees, a new heading should be calculated as shown in the next paragraph.

Estimation of Wind Effect

On Groundspeed: The maximum effect of windspeed is felt when

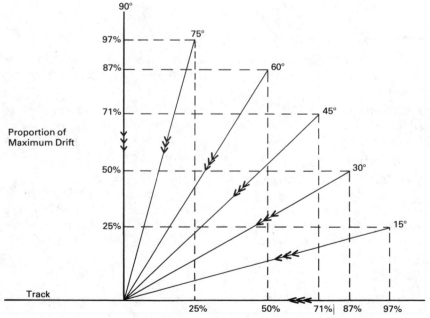

Proportion of Wind Strength Affecting Ground Speed.

the wind direction is from ahead or astern of track and decreases to approximately zero on the beam.

On Drift: Similarly, the angle of wind to track may be expressed as a factor of the maximum possible drift resulting when the wind is on the beam. Maximum drift is determined by the 1:60 rule using the windspeed and airspeed vectors. The maximum drift is then reduced by the factor for the wind direction involved. When the drift is known, the course to steer can be calculated to make good the particular track required. These calculations are only approximations but are acceptable in pilot navigation.

Estimation of Distance

Constant practice on the ground in mental estimation of distances on maps of various scales is necessary to improve accuracy.

Hand Measurements: The span of the hand from thumb to little finger will provide a reliable measure if its dimension is known in terms of the scales of maps used. The distance from thumbnail to knuckle crease is useful for shorter distances.

Parallels of Latitude: On a map these provide useful visual aids to distance measuring.

Estimation of Direction

As with estimation of distance, constant practice is necessary to improve accuracy and this can be assisted by use of the following methods:

Bisecting the Angle: Having decided in which quadrant the required track lies, the angle can then be estimated quite accurately by progressively halving the sector in which it lies and finally interpolating between the estimated 'bracket lines'.

Graduated Pencil: With a graduated pencil, mark off a set number of units along a latitude line from the position of intersection of track with the latitude line. From the same start point measure the set number of units along track. Measure the distance between the two points with reference to the graduated pencil. Double the distance for angular measurement.

Speed Adjustment

When running late and a correction of TAS is required, the following formula is useful:

Additional TAS required $= \dfrac{\text{TAS x Time late on ETA}}{\text{Actual time to go to ETA}}$

When running ahead of time, speed reduction is the obvious answer.

Map Analysis

Every pilot should be familiar with the general properties of the various types of maps and symbols used. In map analysis however, the process is carried a step further and attention is given to whole areas along the route, assessing in detail the various features thereon, so that a full mental picture can be built up.

When extracting detailed information, a logical sequence of analysis is necessary. The following is an example:

> General location
> Relief
> Coastlines and Water features
> Agricultural and Built-up areas
> Communications
> Special features

General Location: Under this heading the general aspects are considered – whether the area is coastal or inland, whether flat or hilly, etc. This will consist of dividing into sections the countryside over which the route passes. Within each section, countryside having the same general characteristics will be shown.

Relief: This is well portrayed on nearly all maps by contour lines or layer tinting. When low flying, it is possible to obtain pinpoints from hills, valleys, etc., so that a closer study becomes necessary. The approach should then be as follows:

> Are the hills in ranges, if so, what is their direction?
> Are the slopes steep or shallow?
> What are the minimum and maximum heights of the ground?
> Are the valleys steep and broad or just shallow indentations?

Coastline and Water Features: The nature of a coastline is important; cliffs, sand dunes, and widths and nature of beaches being outstanding features. Lakes are very distinctive landmarks being recognizable by the shape, position of islands and surroundings (marshes, forests, etc.). Indentations such as estuaries are excellent fixing features.

Agricultural and Built-up Areas: Again, the general features of the area are studied. The shapes of wooded areas, ploughed or cropped land, and terracing will, if indicated, give the pilot a valuable insight into what to expect when he gets airborne.

Built-up areas also form distinctive landmarks by virtue of their size and shape. Mines, brickworks, churches, cemeteries, etc., are usually indicated on the map and provide easily recognizable pinpoints.

Communications: Roads and railways almost invariably lead into important focal areas and their patterns are useful. Single and double tracks, embankments and cuttings, bridges and tunnels, are all aids to identification. Bypasses, bridges, traffic islands, etc., should also be noted to complete the mental picture.

Special Features: This covers the remaining miscellaneous features such as airfields, radio stations, power lines, oilfields, lighthouses, etc.

MAP READING

There are four basic factors upon which the success of map reading depends:

> Knowledge of direction
> Knowledge of distance
> Identification of features
> Selection of landmarks

Direction: The first action in map reading is to orientate the map. By doing so the pilot relates the direction of land features to their representations on the map and so aids recognition.

Distance: When the map has been properly orientated it becomes easier to compare distances between landmarks on the ground with their corresponding distances on the map, thus facilitating the fixing of position.

Anticipation of Landmarks: In pre-flight planning, the relationship of easily recognizable features to the intended track is noted and a time established at which the helicopter will be in their vicinity. Thus, in flight, the pilot is prepared to make his visual observation at a particular time, avoiding undue diversions of attention from other details of the flight.

Check Features and Priority Selection: The basic principle governing the selection of best check features is the ease with which they can be identified. They must be readily distinguishable from their surroundings. The conspicuousness of any check features depends on:

Angle of Observation: At low levels, features are more easily recognized from their outline in elevation rather than in plan. As altitude is increased, the plan outline becomes more important.

Uniqueness of the Feature: To avoid ambiguity, the ideal feature should be the only one of its particular outline in the vicinity.

Contrast and Colour: These properties play a large part in the identification of a particular feature. Map reading may be complicated by seasonal variations.

Fixing by Map Reading

Map reading techniques are largely dependant upon the weather and are evolved for:

Conditions which permit continuous visual observations of the ground.

Conditions which limit visual observations of the ground to unpredictable intervals.

Map Reading in Continuous Conditions: By means of a time scale on track, graduated to groundspeed, the pilot can be prepared to look for a definite feature at a definite time. As a check on identification, other ground detail surrounding the feature should be positively recognized.
THUS, WHEN IN CONTINUOUS CONTACT WITH THE GROUND, READ FROM MAP TO GROUND.

Map Reading at Unpredictable Intervals: This technique increases when flying through broken cloud or descending through it. The pilot first estimates a circle of uncertainty for his position based on a ten per cent error of the distance flown from his last known position. As a steady heading is maintained, the circle of uncertainty will move along with the estimated DR position, increasing in diameter. The pilot then studies the ground features over which he is passing, noting outstanding features and the sequence in which they occur. He then attempts to identify these features on his map within the circle of uncertainty and establish his position and track made good.
THUS, WHEN SEEKING TO ESTABLISH POSITION, READ FROM GROUND TO MAP.

PLANNING THE LOW LEVEL FLIGHT

It is impossible to complete detailed planning successfully without a comprehensive realization of what the flight involves. The main point to consider at this stage is the best route to be followed after considering the following factors:

Mountain Ranges and High Ground: Mountain ranges and high ground are generally associated with changeable weather and turbulence making pinpointing difficult. Intense concentration is required to maintain constant altitude over rugged terrain.

Bad Weather Areas: Areas of poor visibility are likely to be encountered downwind of industrial areas and should be avoided.

Length of Flight: Indirect routing should never be overdone at the expense of a reasonable safety margin of fuel.

Direction of Sun: It is very easy to overshoot landmarks when flying into sun. Obstacles obscured by glare may be quite hazardous. Flying up-sun in industrial haze makes map reading from low level difficult.

Weather: The most carefully laid plans and calculations are easily upset by unexpected changes in the forecast weather. However, such changes need not upset the pilot who possesses a sound knowledge of weather in general and local weather in particular. When flying in conditions of poor visibility care should be taken not to loose visual contact with the ground.

PROCEDURE WHEN UNCERTAIN OF POSITION

The procedure to be adopted by the pilot when he is uncertain of his position cannot be laid down as a series of hard and fast rules. It varies with each individual case.

A pilot who has two way communication with the ground should, if at all uncertain of his position, make full use of available DF and Fixing facilities BEFORE it is too late for assistance to be given.

No VHF Contact: Occasion may arise when VHF contact cannot be made and in the absence of other radio facilities, the pilot is unable to fix himself by reference to the ground. The subsequent action depends on numerous factors including weather, terrain, the type and endurance of the helicopter, always bearing in mind the primary aim which is:

THE SUCCESSFUL COMPLETION OF THE FLIGHT OR, FAILING THIS, THE SAFE LANDING OF THE AIRCRAFT.

In general, the following guiding principles prevail:

Safety: Check safety altitude and fuel remaining.

Why are you lost?: Check compass reading, airspeed, W/V if possible and operation of watch.

Action:
Lost, in visual contact with ground and likely to remain in contact: Fly for endurance. Turn towards the nearest unique line feature. Review DR position by taking into account all factors which may have affected it. On the way to the line feature attempt to fix position by map reading, using the techniques described earlier. When position is established, decide whether destination or diversion is within range.

Lost, no visual contact established without going below safety altitude: Depending on the prevailing weather, locality and remaining fuel, fly for range towards the most suitable area for descent (generally over the sea), and when within this area descend to the minimum safe altitude. The ETA at this area should be calculated depending on the DR error since the last fix.

If contact is established over the sea, fly back towards the coast.

If minimum safe altitude is reached without making contact, climb to the safety altitude, make allowance for the DR error, and fly to an area suitable for abandoning the aircraft.

IT IS ESSENTIAL TO ALLOW SUFFICIENT TIME FOR THE PROCEDURE TO HAVE A REASONABLE CHANCE OF COMPLETION AND ACTION MUST NEVER, IN ANY CIRCUM-STANCE, BE DELAYED.

ENVIRONMENTAL FLIGHT

Excessive aircraft noise can result not only in discomfort and inconvenience but in the possibility of having mandatory flying restrictions imposed over certain areas of the countryside. It is particularly undesirable near built-up areas, schools, hospitals, churches and outdoor assemblies of people.

Reaction to helicopter noise will be adverse and strong if the sound is too irritating or represents something that seems to threaten safety.

Although many commercial operators include environmental flying in their operating manuals, it is up to all helicopter pilots to fly in such a way as to make the sound of their helicopter as acceptable as possible.

NOISE LEVELS

The noise level of a light helicopter (5000 lbs gross weight or less) is a function of the type of engine fitted.

Turbine engined helicopters are quieter than piston engined ones and produce sounds no louder than surface transportation vehicles.

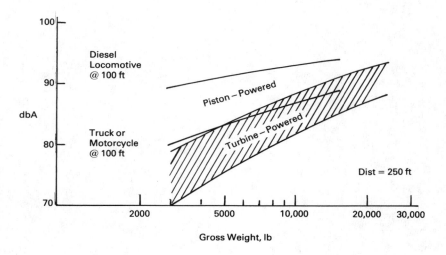

Trend of Helicopter Noise Levels (dbA Units).

Notice that the noise level of a helicopter at a given gross weight covers a certain range. This is true not only for helicopters in general but also for a particular helicopter type.

Therefore, what you need to know is how you can fly your particular type of helicopter in the lower portion of this range of sound level.

SOURCE OF HELICOPTER SOUND

The acoustical signature of a helicopter is partly due to the modulation of sound by the relatively slow turning main rotor.

This modulated sound is often referred to as '**blade slap**'.

For a typical light helicopter, blade slap occurs during partial power descents when one rotor blade intersects its own vortex system or that of another blade. When this happens, the blade experiences high velocities and rapid angle of attack changes. This can drive a section of the rotor blade into compressibility and possibly shock stall, both of which produce aerodynamic loading variations. Either or both generate sound.

A chart of noisy (blade slap) regions shown as functions of airspeed, rate of climb and rate of descent is shown below and indicates where you can expect to produce the most sound in a light helicopter.

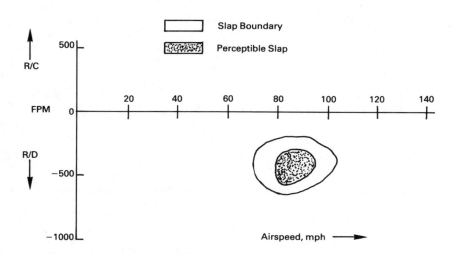

Noisy Flight Operations – Light Helicopters.

Maximum blade slap occurs at airspeeds of sixty-five to eighty-five kts and rates of descent between 300 and 600 feet per minute.

The 'slap boundary' for your own particular type of helicopter may be somewhat different than that shown because the main rotor may slap intermittently when it encounters wind gusts or if you transition rapidly from one flight condition to another.

Although the sound produced does not seem extremely loud to the pilot it can be heard and used to define the slap boundaries for the particular type of helicopter.

Of course, people on the ground hear the noise more readily and notice the blade slap increase in intensity as the helicopter descends.

HOW TO MINIMIZE NOISE

In general, you can eliminate the most offensive sounds by flying outside of the blade slap regions for your particular helicopter. When this is not possible they should be flown through as quickly as possible.

There are other methods of reducing helicopter noise, which you should use whether you are flying in the slap region or not.

Routes and Airspeeds

1. Fly at highest practical altitude during approach to built-up areas.
2. Select a route into your landing site over the least populated area.
3. Avoid low flying over residential areas.
4. Maintain as high a cruising speed as possible.
5. Select final approach with due regard to the type of area surrounding the landing point.

Noise Abatement Approach and Landing

1. When commencing final approach, follow one of these two procedures:
Establish a good rate of descent **before** reducing airspeed, or
Hold rate of descent below 200 fpm whilst reducing airspeed to about 60 kts, then increase rate of descent.
2. At a convenient airspeed between fifty and eighty kts, establish required angle of approach whilst maintaining a good rate of descent.

3. Increase rate of descent if main rotor tends to slap.

4. Approaching the flare, reduce airspeed to below sixty kts before decreasing rate of descent.

The basic difference between this approach technique and a normal one is that this avoids the blade slap region. Both techniques give approximately the same airspeed during the approach, with the quieter technique using an approach angle which is a few degrees steeper.

Once the pilot has transitioned from cruise and established his approach angle, he can then adjust his airspeed and rate of descent to suit local conditions whilst operating at minimum noise.

Departure

Transitions into the climb-out are reasonably quiet operations. You can limit the total ground area exposed to helicopter noise by using a high rate of climb technique and making a very smooth transition.

Your departure route should take you over areas which are the least sensitive to noise.

METEOROLOGICAL CONSIDERATIONS

Wind has two effects on sound. It carries it in the direction toward which it is blowing and it makes a background noise of its own.

In inland areas, surface winds are generally stronger during daytime and weaker at night.

In coastal regions, land and sea breezes give a different diurnal pattern, beginning to blow shortly after sunrise (sea breeze), and sunset (land breeze).

You can use these winds to increase the acceptability of your helicopter by flying **downwind** of densely populated areas and by scheduling after noon the majority of flights near especially noise sensitive areas.

Temperature likewise has two effects on sound. Firstly is the tendency of warm air to be more turbulent than cold air and therefore to disperse sound and decrease its nuisance effect. However, the major effect of temperature depends on the temperature gradient – the change in temperature with altitude.

The normal gradient is negative – temperature decreasing with altitude.

Because sound travels faster in warmer air, in atmosphere with the normal gradient the lower part of a sound wave tends to outrun the upper part, making the propagation, in effect, curve upwards and away from the populace.

The negative gradient reaches a maximum in the late morning or just after noon, and is more intense during summer months. This means that it is of some value to schedule flights to and from noise sensitive areas during warmer times of the day.

At certain times, however, there may be an inversion in the atmosphere – a layer of air in which the temperature **increases** with altitude.

The inversion reverses the normal curvature of sound propagation, turning an abnormally high proportion of the sound energy back towards the ground.

The most severe inversions usually occur at night and in the early morning. These, then, are the times when the sound of the helicopter will have the most adverse effect upon people on the ground.

Although environment is hardly a meteorological subject, it is important to mention here that the ground environment has much to do with the offensiveness of the sound you make with your helicopter.

The background noise level of residential areas is at its lowest point between late evening and early morning. In warm weather, people are apt to be relaxing out of doors in the evenings and at weekends. It is at these times that people are most conscious and resentful of noise intrusion and therefore, it is at these times also that you should be most reluctant to fly noisily.

3

AIR
EXERCISES

GENERAL NOTES FOR STUDENT HELICOPTER PILOTS

These exercises are the approved CAA syllabus for PPL (H) and associated ratings.

1. This study guide has been prepared to supplement the flying and ground instruction.

    It is designed to help you understand more fully your instructor's exercise briefings and in-flight demonstrations.

    Each exercise does not necessarily represent one flying lesson. Some exercises require several flights and sometimes more than one exercise is covered in one lesson. Because of this, you should always be a few exercises ahead in your reading.

    Your instructor will assume that you will have read the relevant exercise(s) prior to attending your flying lesson.

2. **This section provides**

    a) A progressive series of Air Exercises in which the helicopter pilot is required to be proficient.

    b) The main considerations of each exercise that will be stressed during full and pre-flight briefings.

3. **Air Exercises**

    The air exercises are listed under main titles and are numbered from 1–27. The initial flights will be confined to a particular exercise but as the course progresses revision on previous exercises will be done as well as introduction to more advanced exercises.

4. **Principles of Flight**

    The principles of flight for each air exercise are not discussed in this section. Detailed information can be obtained from the section entitled *Principles of Flight* at the beginning of the book. The information given in this handbook, together with ground school instruction, is the foundation upon which your instructor will base your helicopter flying training.

5. **Full Briefings**

    The full briefing is given before each new exercise is taught in the air. As the name suggests this briefing covers the subject in detail. It may take up to an hour to deliver. During this briefing the lessons learnt in the ground school are linked to the practical aspects of flying.

6. Pre-Flight Briefings

Pre-flight briefings will be given just before each flight. As well as including a resume of the main points of the air exercise, the briefing will also cover details which will affect the conduct of the flight, namely weather, airfield state and air traffic control.

7. Post-Flight Discussion

After every dual lesson the flight will be discussed. This discussion will be a review of the exercise and is used to amplify or clarify any particular point or difficulty, thus consolidating the exercise as a whole.

Exercises 1–3   FAMILIARIZATION AND AIR EXPERIENCE

1. **Introduction**

    The Air Experience flight serves to give you an introduction into the new sensations of helicopter flight and also gives your instructor an opportunity to show you the local area. On the ground the instructor will satisfy himself that you are fully briefed and conversant with all the helicopter checks and drills.

2. Airmanship will be stressed throughout the course by your instructor.

3. Your instructor will brief you fully on the safety procedures. The two most important points to remember when approaching the helicopter are:

    a) Only approach the helicopter in the sector where the pilot can see you.

    b) Do not enter the disc area until you receive positive clearance.

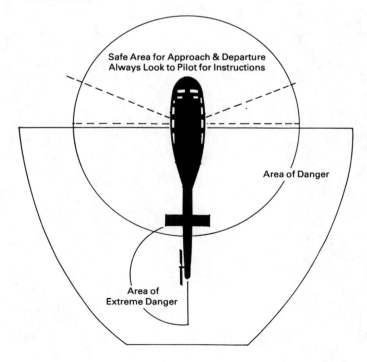

Exercise 4   EFFECTS OF CONTROLS

1.   Introduction

Before you can begin to fly a helicopter it is necessary to fully understand the effects of each control.

2.   Airmanship

During this lesson the helicopter will be climbing and descending and it is therefore of the utmost importance that you keep a good lookout. Whilst maintaining a good lookout you will be expected to keep a check of your position within the local area and also make routine checks of engine temperatures and pressures.

3.   The Controls

a)   **The cyclic stick** controls the helicopter in the horizontal plane. There is no 'feel' and it is not self-centering. Movement of the cyclic in any direction will cause the rotor disc to tilt. This will cause the attitude to alter. For example; movement of the cyclic forward causes the disc to tilt forward and the helicopter to adopt a nose-down attitude, similarly movement of the cyclic to port will result in the helicopter banking to port, and the helicopter will enter a turn.

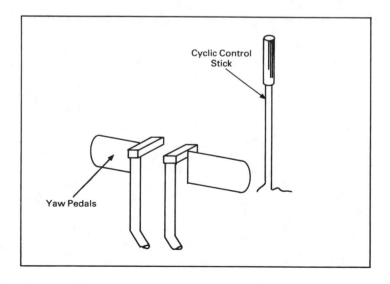

b) **The collective lever** controls the helicopter in the vertical plane. Raising the lever increases the pitch collectively on all the rotor blades which causes an increase in rotor thrust resulting in the helicopter climbing. Increasing the pitch also increases the rotor drag and the rotor RPM will decay. Lowering the lever will have the reverse effect.

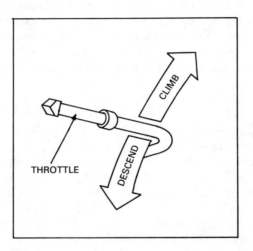

c) **The throttle** twist grip is very sensitive and controls the RPM. As the lever is raised and the RPM starts to fall off, the throttle must be opened to maintain the RPM at a constant figure. As the throttle is opened increasing torque will cause the helicopter to yaw and this must be counteracted with movement of the pedals. Since it is always necessary to open the throttle when the lever is raised in powered flight to maintain RPM, a cam is placed between the lever and the throttle butterfly in the carburettor. As the lever is raised, the throttle butterfly is automatically opened by the cam system to compensate for the increase in rotor drag and help maintain constant RPM. Hence lever movements will cause power changes and the yaw pedals will be needed to maintain the helicopter heading during these torque variations. In practice the mechanical cam system is not perfect and some variations in RPM can be expected as lever movements are made. These must be corrected with the throttle twist grip control.

d) **Yaw pedals** are very sensitive and are used in forward flight to keep the helicopter in balance. Whenever the power is increased, left pedal must be applied to maintain balance and when power is reduced then right pedal must be applied. If the helicopter is flown out of balance, airspeed errors may occur as the pitot tube is being blanked off from the airflow.

4. **Further Effects of Lever and Throttle**

Sometime during the lesson your instructor will demonstrate an autorotation to you. This is achieved by progressively lowering the lever and initially maintaining the RPM within limits. When the lever is finally as far down as it will go, the throttle has to be closed further to keep the RPM within limits and the autorotative state occurs when a needle split is achieved, i.e. the rotor is free-wheeling. The rate of descent increases as the lever is lowered until it reaches a maximum when the aircraft is in autorotation.

5. **Frictions**

To make flying less tiring frictions are provided on some controls. The frictions should be adjusted during the pre-take-off checks to the point at which the controls do not move of their own accord due to vibration or, in the case of the lever, under its own weight. The helicopter is normally flown with the collective friction off.

6. **Instruments**

Of all the instruments, two warrant special mention.

a) **The manifold pressure gauge** gives an indication of engine power. The scale of the gauge is measured in inches of mercury.

b) **The RPM gauge** indicates both engine RPM (the long needle) and the rotor RPM. When the clutch is engaged and the engine is driving the rotor, the two needles will be superimposed. In the event of there being a difference in engine and rotor speeds, e.g. in autorotation, the needles will be split.

7. **Effect of change of Disc Loading**

You will be shown how the RRPM will rise with an increase of positive 'G' and that they will decrease if negative 'G' is applied.

8.   Effect of changes of Airspeed

You will also be shown how airspeed affects RRPM.

Increase in speed	–	RRPM increases
Decrease in speed	–	RRPM decreases

Exercise 5 ATTITUDE AND POWER CHANGES

1. Introduction

In this exercise you will learn the relationship of attitude to airspeed and how to make changes of attitude. You will also learn how to control RPM and make changes of manifold pressure.

2. Airmanship

a) **Lookout.** This exercise will involve the helicopter climbing and descending; it is therefore important to maintain a lookout above and below as well as the same height. You must also note your location throughout your lesson, although at this stage your instructor will help by pointing out local landmarks.

b) **Temperatures and Pressures.** As various power settings are used, it is necessary to make sure at regular intervals that the T's and P's are in the 'GREEN' and that sufficient fuel remains to continue the sortie.

c) **Positive Handover/Takeover.** During the demonstrations, you will be asked to 'follow through on the controls', it is important that you do just that and do not override your instructor. When your instructor wants you to take control, he will say, 'You have control'. You will then take hold of the control(s) and say 'I have control'. The order will be reversed when he requires to re-take control. Never let go of the controls until your instructor has acknowledged as having control.

3. During Flight

a) **Attitude and IAS.** Starting from cruise flight, you will be shown that there is a set attitude for a given airspeed. You will be shown how to change this attitude and therefore change the airspeed. Due to an effect called 'Flapback', which your instructor will explain to you; you will find that as the airspeed changes the attitude will change for the same cyclic stick position. It is therefore necessary to hold the desired attitude by moving the cyclic stick further during the speed change. You will be required to recognize and maintain these attitudes in order to fly at selected speeds.

b) **Changing power at constant RPM.** The height of the helicopter is controlled by the lever which in turn controls the pitch of the rotor blades. As pitch is altered, the engine power (MP) will have to be altered to maintain constant RPM because of the change in the rotor drag. This power change can be effected by either the throttle twist-grip or by the lever operated cam system. It is worth mentioning at this stage that the setting-up of the cam will vary from helicopter to helicopter and therefore its effectiveness will vary. You will probably, therefore, be taught two methods of changing power at constant RPM, they are correlated and uncorrelated methods.

   i) **Uncorrelated Method.** If there were no cam system and the lever was raised, the RPM would decay. To stop this happening the throttle is opened a small amount first, which increases power and RPM. The lever is then raised to reduce the RPM to the original figure and to increase pitch. This method is continued until the required amount of power/pitch is reached and the RPM is still at the original figure. To decrease power, the lever is lowered first and the RPM controlled by closing the throttle slightly until the required amount of power is obtained.

   ii) **Correlated Method.** As the cam will try to maintain RPM, it is often found that the best way to make a power change is to lead with the lever when increasing or decreasing power and then to trim the RPM with the throttle. This is the method you will probably have to use most often.

4. It is important that all your control movements at this stage are slow and small until you are satisfied that you are correct in all your actions. As you become more proficient your instructor will show you how to co-ordinate the use of throttle and lever into a single movement. You will also find that although most of your time is spent looking at the MP and RPM gauges, your instructor will encourage you to maintain a lookout as often as possible by applying a scan sequence, i.e. lookout, instruments, lookout . .

5. **RPM changes at constant MP**

   It will be necessary to change your RPM during the climb or

descent, or when you inadvertently allow them to alter during normal flight.

a) To increase RPM with constant manifold pressure – lead with throttle, resulting not only in increase of RPM but also an increase in manifold pressure. Lower lever until manifold pressure reduces to original value and as a result you will gain a further increase in RPM.

b) To decrease RPM with constant manifold pressure – Lead with throttle, resulting in not only a decrease of RPM but also a decrease in manifold pressure. Raise lever until manifold pressure returns to original figure and as a result your RPM will decrease even further.

Exercise 6 LEVEL FLIGHT, CLIMBING AND DESCENDING INCLUDING TURNS

1. Introduction

The aim of this exercise is to utilize the power and attitude changing techniques we learnt in the previous lesson, to achieve level flight and entries into the climb and descent. These manoeuvres must be practiced until they can be flown accurately and smoothly.

The basic rules to remember are that the **lever** controls **height** and the **cyclic** controls the **attitude** and hence the **airspeed**. Remember also to allow time for the airspeed to stabilize before making further attitude adjustments. Whenever a power change is made it will be necessary to adjust the yaw pedals to keep the helicopter in balance (cross-check the slip indicator) and to maintain a constant heading. Initially, it is a good idea to pick a feature ahead of the helicopter and then to keep it on the nose as the power change is carried out.

As airspeed is varied, both flapback and inflow roll will cause the helicopter's attitude to change without a cyclic stick movement. Although this attitude change will be small, it will be necessary to counteract it with small cyclic movements as the airspeed increases or decreases, in order to maintain the selected attitude.

A good lookout should cover the whole area around the helicopter, but the area into which the helicopter is moving, particularly whilst climbing and descending, is especially important.

2. Level Flight

To achieve level flight, use the visual horizon primarily to maintain the helicopter's attitude, cross-checking to the ASI to ensure that it is the correct attitude for the required airspeed. You will also practice varying the airspeed between 100 and sixty mph, maintaining a constant height. It will be seen from the power Required v TAS graph in the Principles of Flight notes, that less power is required to maintain level flight at sixty mph than at 100 mph, and it will be necessary to adjust the lever position as the attitude change is made to prevent a climb or descent.

Outside Visual References.

3. **Climbing and Descending**

   Entering the Climb from Cruise–APT. From the cruise this is achieved as follows:

   a) Raise nose slightly, selecting the climbing attitude with cyclic (**Attitude** change).

   b) Lead with throttle to maintain RPM and carefully raise the lever to increase power to the required setting. Keep straight with left pedal (**Power** change).

   c) **Trim**.

   d) Make any final adjustments to attitude and power as required.

Climb Attitude.

   Levelling-off from the climb to Cruise–APT. The levelling-off sequence is as follows:

   a) At about fifty feet below the required height (more if the rate of climb is unusually high), select the cruise attitude but do not lower the lever immediately (**Attitude** change).

b) When the helicopter has accelerated lower the lever slightly and reduce throttle setting to cruise power. Keep straight with right pedal (**Power** change).

c) **Trim**.

d) Adjust attitude and power.

Entering the Descent from the Cruise–PAT

a) Lower the lever to initiate a rate of descent. There is no set power figure for the descent since it will depend on the rate of descent required. Maintain RPM and keep straight with pedals (**Power**).

b) Selected descent attitude (**Attitude** change).

c) Adjust power and attitude.

d) **Trim**.

Levelling from Descent to the Cruise–PAT

a) Anticipate slightly your arrival at the required height and increase power to cruise setting. Keep straight with pedals (**Power**).

b) Select cruise attitude (**Attitude** change).

c) Adjust power and attitude.

d) **Trim**.

4. Turning

Level fifteen degree bank turns maintaining attitude and angle of bank with the stick will be practised. In a sustained turn power will have to be increased to maintain height. Fifteen degree bank turns will also be practiced in the climb and descent. It will be noticed that large angles of bank will decrease the rate of climb and increase the rate of descent. Yaw pedal will be required to maintain balance in the turns and left and right turns will appear to have different attitudes due to the offset seats.

Attitude During Left and Right Turns.

5. Conclusion

After a good deal of practice the above exercise should become smooth, co-ordinated movements of all controls simultaneously but in the initial stages, remember the sequences laid down in section 1.

Exercise 7 BASIC AUTOROTATIONS

1. Introduction

In powered flight the rotor drag is overcome by engine power but if the engine fails, or is deliberately disengaged from the rotor system, some other force must be used to maintain the rotor RPM. This is achieved by allowing the helicopter to descend by lowering the collective lever so that the resultant airflow strikes the blade in such a manner that the airflow itself provides the driving force. When the helicopter descends in this manner, the rate of descent becomes the power equivalent and the helicopter is said to be in a state of **AUTOROTATION**.

2. Attitude Change on Entry and Recovery

On entry into autorotation the nose will tend to pitch down. The airflow in powered flight is flowing over the rotor disc and is induced down through it. In autorotation, the airflow is coming up from underneath and striking the elevator/tail stabilizer causing the nose to pitch down.

On recovery from autorotation to the climb the tendency will be for the nose to pitch up. This is more critical as a nose-up pitch will result in a loss of airspeed from the already low airspeed. At this stage of the recovery full power is being applied whilst the aircraft has a high rate of descent. The combination of these factors could lead to a dangerous condition of flight known as Vortex Ring should the helicopter also have a low airspeed.

3. Vortex Ring

For the helicopter to get into Vortex Ring, three factors are required simultaneously:

a)   A high rate of descent.

b)   Low airspeed, below twenty-five knots.

c)   High power setting.

4. Inflow Roll

Inflow roll is the phenomenon which causes the helicopter to roll slightly to the right in powered flight. The pilot moves the cyclic stick slightly to the left to correct this tendency – usually the basic student is unaware that he has made this correction as it is very small. On entry into autorotation inflow roll decreases and unless the student maintains the attitude laterally with the cyclic, the aircraft will roll to the left. This will be demonstrated by your instructor.

5. Basic Autorotation

The basic autorotation is practiced at sixty mph with the lever lowered fully. To enter autorotation, the lever must be lowered while closing the throttle to prevent the engine overspeeding. The engine RPM and the rotor RPM needles should still be together on the tachometer until the lever is fully down. Simultaneous with this action, the nose must be smoothly raised to the sixty mph attitude and the lateral attitude must be kept level to prevent a roll to port. When the lever is fully down, throttle back to 2000 ERPM. This is called 'splitting the needles'. You are now in autorotation. As power is taken off during the entry, a lot of right pedal must be applied in order to keep the helicopter in balance and on a constant heading.

It is now possible to change airspeed and direction during the descent, height permitting. Increase in airspeed, all-up weight, or disc loading (i.e. positive G) will cause an increase in rotor RPM. Medium turns can be carried out quite simply by use of the cyclic in order to manoeuvre the helicopter into the wind.

To recover to the climb start at about 300 feet before the minimum height for recovery. A small check up on the lever may first be required to ensure that when the needles are joined the engine is not oversped. Open the throttle gently but positively to re-join the needles. When the needles are joined, raise the lever, opening the throttle at the same time to maintain RPM until climb power is reached. Remember the nose tends to pitch up during this large application of power so apply forward cyclic to maintain climb speed. Maintain balance and heading by applying left pedal during the recovery.

6. Airmanship and Limitations

HASEL is the password to good airmanship:

H   Height sufficient to allow recovery by 500 feet AGL if away from the AIRFIELD.
A   Area is suitable.
S   Security, harnesses, no loose articles.
E   Engine Check T's and P's.
L   Lookout – maintain a lookout all round and especially below for other aircraft. A lookout on recovery is also very important.

Also check the wind velocity and ensure that the area you are going to use is suitable should your practice become real. The precautions in the E of HASEL are designed to prevent embarrassing engine cut-backs.

Exercise 8   HOVERING

1. Introduction

The aim of this exercise is to teach you how to hover; that is to maintain a given position relative to the ground at a constant height, heading and RPM. The hover is a basic requirement in helicopter flying since it is the prerequisite to safe landings and is also the basic factor in many operational functions.

2. Hovering

The helicopter will normally hover with the left skid low. This is caused by the correction for tail rotor drift. The amount by which the left skid hangs low is also dependent on two other factors:

a)   The lateral centre of gravity.

b)   The wind strength and its direction relative to the helicopter.

If both the left and right hand seats are occupied, then the left skid will probably only be one to two inches lower than the right, whereas if only the left hand seat is occupied then the left skid may be as much as six inches lower than the right.

At this stage in your training all hovering will be done into wind. The helicopter will tend to drift downwind if no corrective action is taken so to maintain a position relative to the ground the disc must be tilted into wind and this will result in a change in the hover attitude.

If the wind velocity were to change this would cause variations in the amount of drift which could be corrected by cyclic pitch. There would also be variations in translational lift which would cause the helicopter to climb or descend, this could be corrected by use of the collective lever. In general the helicopter will tend to climb and move away from any gust of wind.

In still air conditions, a ground cushion is formed, the intensity of which cushion depends on the hover height and the nature of the ground.

In the hover the helicopter is statically stable since it will return through its original position if displaced by an outside force, i.e. a gust of wind. However, it will continue through this position and then continue to oscillate about it in increasing amounts. Therefore the helicopter is said to be dynamically unstable in the hover.

3. **Airmanship**

The points of airmanship relevant to hovering are:

a) Lookout – a good lookout all round must be maintained.

b) A large area should be selected without any obstructions.

c) The wind velocity should be noted.

d) Temperatures and pressures should be monitored frequently.

e) Care must be taken not to exceed the power limitations.

f) The procedure for handing/taking over control must be strictly observed.

4. **The Air Exercises**

The exercise will take place heading into wind, four to six feet skid clearance. The functions of each control are as follows:

a) **The cyclic** controls the disc attitude and hence the helicopter attitude and the position of the helicopter over the ground. Small movements only are required and it must be remembered there is a lag between selecting an attitude, the helicopter adopting the new attitude and the resultant helicopter movement.

b) **The collective** controls the height of the helicopter and only small movements of the lever are required.

c) **The throttle** is used to maintain the RPM and again only small movements are required. Check the RPM and manifold pressure gauges.

d) **The yaw pedals** are used to control the helicopter's direction and operate in the normal sense, e.g. applying left pedal turns the nose of the helicopter to the left.

In order to maintain an accurate hover it is necessary for the pilot to determine whether or not he is maintaining his position over the ground at a given height, on a given heading and constant RPM. A good scan is required which should include the following points:

a) A mid-distance object some seventy-five to 100 yards ahead to gain a general perspective.

b) The visual horizon for attitude and heading.

c) Markers ahead and to the side to determine accurate position and height.

d) Frequent reference to the RPM and manifold pressure gauges.

In the hover there is a tendency to stare at a fixed point and thus the pilot is denying himself the other reference points which help him to maintain a hover. It is suggested that a good scan be evolved which involves looking at external references for seventy-five per cent of the time and referring to instruments for the remaining twenty-five per cent.

Exercise 9   LANDINGS AND TAKE-OFFS

1. Introduction

Landings are normally taught before take-offs as they are a direct follow-on from hovering. Unless you can hover steadily, you cannot possibly expect to be able to land with any degree of success. A good landing therefore starts from a steady hover.

2. Landings

The first requirement is a steady hover at four to six feet, heading into wind. Then, looking well ahead to maintain the attitude, the lever is slowly and steadily lowered to put the helicopter on the ground. The best way to achieve this initially is to make a very small movement of the lever and wait to see its effect. In all probability we will now be hovering at, say, three to four feet and a further small lever movement should reduce our hover height even more. Continue until the skids touch the ground. Maintain a look-out well ahead of the helicopter during the landing and make a positive effort to relax.

During this period the RPM are maintained by gentle use of the throttle. Any movement of lever or throttle will affect the torque and so the helicopter must be kept straight with the pedals, hence once again the necessity to look ahead. As the helicopter gets closer to the ground, the natural left skid low attitude of the helicopter becomes more apparent and any tendency to level the helicopter with right cyclic must be avoided. It will be noted, therefore, that the helicopter lands left skid first. When this happens, continue to lower the lever gently. The right skid will then touch. Continue to gently lower the lever all the way to the bottom stop. This will require a certain amount of throttle closing to prevent the RPM from exceeding their limits.

When the lever is fully down and it is apparent that the helicopter is firmly on the ground, the after landing checks are carried out; these are:

a) Throttle   –   Set idling RPM

b) Lever   –   Fully down, friction on

c) Cyclic   –   Disc level and trimmed

d) Pedals   –   Neutral

The frictions are omitted if we are doing a sequence of take-offs and landings and are about to take-off again.

In the event of any form of mis-landing, do not waffle around in close proximity to the ground, apply power and climb back up to the four to six feet hover, settle down and try again.

3. Take-offs

Carry out the pre-take-off checks as detailed in the checklist. Before attempting to take-off note the wind direction. Position the cyclic so that the helicopter will lift off with no lateral movement over the ground. In a strong wind, the cyclic will be positioned further forward than in calm conditions. The yaw pedals can also be pre-positioned before take-off. The amount of pedal required will depend on the power used to take-off and will vary with the weight of the helicopter and the wind velocity, but normally it is with the left pedal just slightly ahead of the right.

Vertical Take-off to a Hover.

Having pre-set the controls, open the throttle gently to set flying RPM and look outside to ensure that everything is clear in the vicinity of the helicopter. Increase power smoothly, maintaining RPM; as the helicopter is about to lift off, see if there were any inaccuracies in the pre-positioning of the cyclic and pedals by the helicopter sliding or yawing on the ground. Whilst continuing to increase power, correct for these inaccuracies as the helicopter leaves the ground. Still continue to increase power, maintaining heading and RPM until the helicopter has climbed to the hover height of four to six feet. Having settled in the hover, carry out the after-take-off checks:

a) Controls — Normal operation and Trimmed

b) Manifold Pressure — Note M.P. required for hovering

c) RPM — Correctly Set

d) T's and P's — Within limits

Exercise 10   TRANSITIONS

1. Introduction

Up to now you have flown the helicopter in two entirely different conditions of flight; in 'conventional' situations above fifty mph, and operating in the ground cushion. The time has come to join the two together. It will help at this stage if the various factors that affect the helicopter in the transition are understood. First, let us look at the factors that affect the power requirements of the helicopter:

a) **Ground Cushion.** We know from the hovering exercise that less power is required to hover at four feet than, say, thirty feet and also that any fore and aft or lateral movement of the helicopter will disturb the ground cushion so that more power will be required to maintain height.

b) **Vertical component of total rotor thrust.** Simply stated, if we tilt the rotor thrust vector to provide a component to move the helicopter forward, then less is available to hold the helicopter up and it will sink unless we provide a larger rotor thrust by raising the lever and increasing the power.

c) **Flapback.** If we let the speed of the helicopter increase, but hold the stick position fixed, then, as a result of dissymmetry of lift (more lift on the advancing side), the blades will flap to equality. This phenomenon is covered more deeply in *The Principles of Flight*. Thus as speed builds up the stick will have to be moved forward to maintain a constant helicopter attitude.

d) **Translational Lift.** *The Principles of Flight* covers the subject in more detail – sufficient to say here that as helicopter forward speed increases above about twenty mph less power is required to maintain height.

2. Transitions

As we have said, the transition is one of the basic helicopter exercises and it is obviously important to master the principles thoroughly in the academic exercise so that subsequent and more advanced exercises can be tackled with confidence. We split the exercise into three phases, each of which will be discussed separately. These are:

a) The transition from the hover into forward flight and back to the hover.

b) The transition from the hover to the climb.

c) The transition from the approach to the hover.

In all cases the main airmanship points are:

a) Thorough lookout along the intended flight path as well as behind the helicopter.

b) Area clear of obstructions and reasonably level.

c) All checks should be carried out at the appropriate times.

d) The wind strength and direction.

Transition from the hover to the hover. This manoeuvre comprises a take-off to a high hover, a clearing turn left to check behind, re-establish the hover and then gently accelerating the helicopter to thirty to forty mph. When the steady state has been achieved the helicopter is then brought back to the hover. We will look at the controls one at a time.

a) **Cyclic.** Ease the helicopter from the hover into a very small nose-down attitude and then hold it. Remember that because of flapback you will have to move the stick forward slightly as you gain speed. Establish the steady state by reducing the nose-down attitude as you reach about thirty-five mph. To re-establish the hover the process is reversed. Raise the nose slightly to slow down and hold it until you almost lose forward speed, then select the hover attitude.

b) **Collective.** As you move off the ground cushion you will need more power until you gain translational lift. Power can then be reduced to maintain this height. As you slow down, the procedure is reversed, but remember to anticipate your increased power requirements as you lose translational lift and make all changes slowly. This will help RPM control.

c) **Yaw.** Keep the helicopter straight. You will be surprised by the large amount of left pedal required as you re-establish the hover so anticipate it.

Transition from the Hover to the Climb. Start from a four foot hover and move into forward flight as described above except that, when you have gained translational lift, apply climb power and allow the helicopter to accelerate before selecting the climb attitude. A common fault is to let the helicopter climb too quickly and put the helicopter into the AVOID AREA.

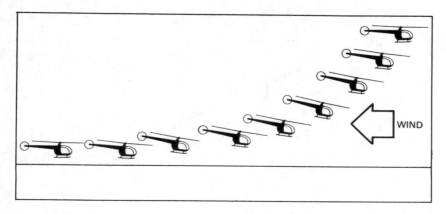

Transition from the Approach to the Hover. The ultimate aim of this lesson is to fly a constant angle of approach to the hover. The angle of the approach will be varied in later exercises, but at the moment you will be taught to approach at about ten degrees. Fly the helicopter level at 400 feet and sixty mph until the correct angle and 'sight picture' is achieved. This will be demonstrated by your instructor. Lower the lever to initiate a rate of descent aiming to keep the same 'sight picture' and hence the same angle of approach. At the same time adopt a slight nose up attitude to reduce speed gradually during the approach, aiming for zero forward speed over the intended hover point. Adjustments to the angle of approach are made by the lever. Corrections will be needed if the 'sight picture' changes – if you are getting low the aspect of the aiming point flattens out – if you are too high the aspect deepens – all this will be demonstrated to you. In the early stages of the approach the aiming point will stay in the same position on the windshield but as the speed decreases the nose will rise and the aiming point will move downwards **To maintain the constant angle of approach the sight picture does not alter.** In the latter stages of the approach the aiming point will disappear beneath the nose, and to ensure you arrive over the aiming point in the hover it is essential that lateral markers are used. Once again this will be demonstrated to you.

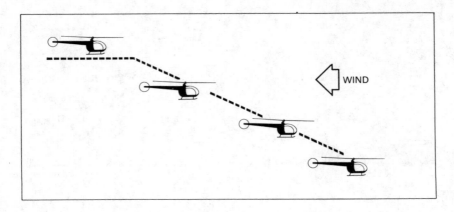

Going through the controls individually:

a) **Cyclic.** Select slight nose up attitude after the rate of descent is established. Remember that flapback will mean that the stick will have to be moved aft to maintain the attitude as speed reduces. Adjust attitude with very small cyclic changes to progressively reduce ground speed to zero over the landing point.

b) **Collective.** Replace translational lift with power using the technique described above to stay on correct approach path. Gentle changes mean easy RPM control.

c) **Yaw.** Keep straight, and remember lots of left pedal at the end of the approach.

3. Conclusion

During these exercises avoid the more common mistakes, which are:

a) Not maintaining a constant angle on the approach.

b) High rates of descent at low airspeed on the approach.

c) Allowing RPM to vary during power changes.

Exercise 11   CIRCUITS

1.   Introduction

The training circuit is designed to combine most of the previous exercises. You should try to fly the heights and speeds as accurately as possible.

Remember that the whole point of the circuit is to enable you to bring the helicopter into a position from which a precisely flown constant angle of approach to a touchdown point can be made.

2.   Airmanship

A good lookout is particularly important during this exercise AND IS MORE IMPORTANT THAN PURE FLYING ACCURACY.

The angle of the final approach must be selected by the pilot for each particular set of circumstances. THERE IS NO ONE 'CORRECT' APPROACH ANGLE, e.g. when landing in a very small clearing it could be a vertical descent with an approach angle of ninety degrees. You must therefore practice approaches at a variety of angles. It is for this reason that the helicopter is flown level at 400 feet and sixty mph after the turn from base leg on to finals. Do not fall into the trap of accepting whatever angle is presented to you as you roll into the final turn or you will get into the habit of flying only one approach angle – and that will be a flat one. Fly level at 400 feet and sixty mph, select your angle and then begin the descent.

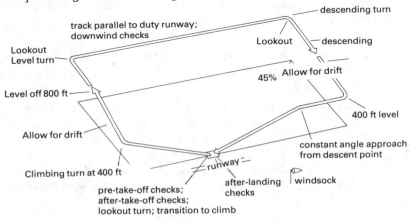

The Standard Training Circuit.

A high rate of descent at low airspeed must be avoided (as there is a danger of VORTEX RING). A maximum rate of descent of 300 feet per minute must not be exceeded below twenty mph airspeed.

You must overshoot if the rate of descent exceeds 300 feet per min below twenty mph or if you are too high or too low in the latter stages of the approach.

Overshoot action is:

a) Stick forward to increase airspeed.

b) Apply climb power.

c) Adopt sixty mph attitude and climb away.

d) Keep a good lookout.

3. Emergencies

Engine off landing procedures have been shown to you at the end of virtually every lesson. Although EOLs are covered later in the course, it is important that you should be able to cope with an engine failure in the circuit before you fly solo.

a) **Engine failure in the hover.** DO NOT LOWER THE LEVER but control the yaw with the right pedal and the roll with the cyclic. Allow the helicopter to sink until at a skid height of about two feet raise the lever sharply to cushion the touchdown.

b) **In the transition.** The same principles apply on the approach and in the climb. If you have the height lower the lever fully. Otherwise level the helicopter and run on preventing yaw and cushioning the touchdown with the lever.

c) **Downwind or crosswind.** Enter autorotation and turn into wind. Select a landing area and carry out the forced landing checks.

d) **Variable flare EOL.** Fly the helicopter in autorotation at sixty mph and at between 75–100 ft AGL establish a decelerative attitude by flaring gently. Hold the attitude and at about twenty-five feet check with lever. At ten to fifteen feet skid height level the helicopter and start to use the lever to cushion the touchdown, ensuring that there is no drift.

Exercise 12 FIRST SOLO FLIGHT

Your first solo flight in the helicopter is an important and exciting occasion.

When your instructor has satisfied himself that you are ready to fly solo he will brief you on exactly what to do.

Normally the flight will consist of a take-off to the hover, a standard training circuit and a landing back at the take-off point. Remember that if you are unhappy with your final approach you should overshoot and go round for another circuit.

First solo flight can easily make you apprehensive but please be reassured – your instructor would not have authorised the flight unless he was absolutely sure of your ability.

The flight will be carefully supervised with your instructor remaining at the take-off point to observe the flight.

For subsequent solo flights you must continue to fly only as briefed.

Experiment with insufficient knowledge can be fatal.

Exercise 13   SIDEWAYS AND BACKWARDS FLIGHT

1.   Introduction

The ability to fly sideways and backwards for short but precise distances is required in most helicopter roles. A little time may be needed to become familiar with the new sensations of flying sideways and backwards over the ground.

2.   Airmanship

a) **Lookout.** It is particularly important that the area behind the helicopter must checked 'clear' before backwards flight.

b) **Speed.** Sideways and backwards flight is recommended to be limited to twenty mph in still air.

c) **Wind.** Initially the exercise will be carried out into wind – only when you are proficient at this will out of wind manoeuvres be demonstrated.

d) **T's and P's.** As prolonged high power will be required, T's and P's must be monitored frequently.

e) **Carbon Monoxide.** When hovering, the heater must not be used.

3.   Sideways Flight (heading into wind)

a) Lookout – particularly in the direction of intended movement.

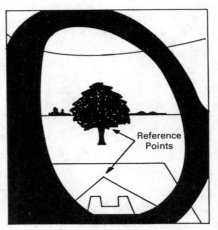

Maintaining Ground Track.

b) Make a SMALL stick movement in the direction required.

c) As attitude changes the helicopter will start to move.

d) Maintain the height with lever.

e) Maintain heading with pedals.

f) Maintain SLOW SPEED over the ground with CYCLIC.

g) To stop, re-select the hover attitude and let the helicopter slowly drift into the hover. Apply power as necessary to hold hover height.

4. Backwards Flight (heading into wind)

a) Lookout – turn the helicopter through ninety degrees and check 'all clear' behind.

b) Before moving backwards CLIMB TO HIGHER HOVER AND REMEMBER THE TAIL ROTOR!

c) Make a small backward movement of the cyclic to get a SLIGHT NOSE UP ATTITUDE.

d) As attitude changes the helicopter will begin to move.

e) Maintain height with lever.

g) Maintain SLOW SPEED with CYCLIC.

h) To stop – re-select the hover attitude.

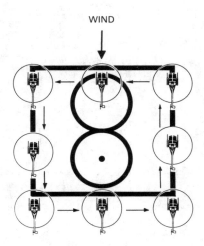

Constant–Heading Square.

5. Dangers

a) Excessive sideways speed can lead to loss of control.

b) Severe nose down pitching during recovery from too fast backwards flight will be demonstrated by your instructor.

6. Sideways and Backwards Flight Heading Out of Wind

Before attempting to move backwards or sideways heading out of wind, hold the helicopter steady in the out of wind hover. Check the following

a) Position of cyclic.

b) Position of yaw pedals.

c) Helicopter attitude.

d) Wind velocity.

Remember that when the helicopter is heading out of wind it will tend to yaw back into wind because of weathercock action. This must be prevented by yaw pedals, and height maintained with power. Control height and speed must be kept within laid down limits.

Having mastered sideways and backwards flight you should now be able to use a combination of these techniques to fly the helicopter in any given direction, in and out of wind and holding any given heading.

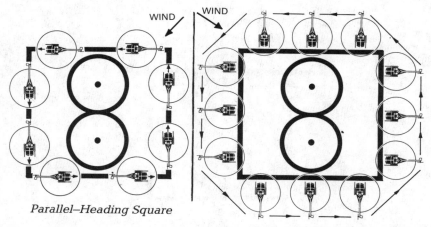

Parallel–Heading Square

Perpendicular–Heading Square

Exercise 14   SPOT TURNS

1. Introduction

This exercise concludes the basic manoeuvres in the ground cushion. Combined with sideways and backwards flight, spot turns will give you complete freedom of movement when operating in ground effect.

2. First of all you will be shown the crosswind and downwind hovers and note the change in cyclic position and helicopter attitude, manifold pressure and your pedal position on the various headings. You will already be familiar with the crosswind as this is used as a 'Lookout turn' during transitions and circuit flying.

3. You will then be shown the action to take if, when hovering downwind, you find the cyclic against the rear stops and the helicopter is drifting downwind. In this situation you should check any drift with pedal and make a gentle run on landing.

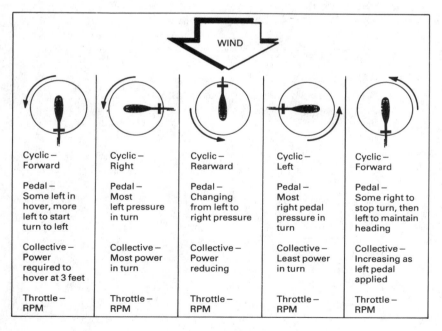

Cyclic – Forward	Cyclic – Right	Cyclic – Rearward	Cyclic – Left	Cyclic – Forward
Pedal – Some left in hover, more left to start turn to left	Pedal – Most left pressure in turn	Pedal – Changing from left to right pressure	Pedal – Most right pedal pressure in turn	Pedal – Some right to stop turn, then left to maintain heading
Collective – Power required to hover at 3 feet	Collective – Most power in turn	Collective – Power reducing	Collective – Least power in turn	Collective – Increasing as left pedal applied
Throttle – RPM	Throttle – RPM	Throttle – RPM	Throttle – RPM	Throttle – RPM

Hovering Left Turn.

4. Having revised hovering you will then carry out a spot turn but stopping the turn every ninety degrees. Note that the basic controls are the yaw pedals, but co-ordinated use of the other controls will be required to maintain a constant position over the ground, together with constant height and RPM.

5. The helicopter's weathercock stability will cause a noticeable increase in the rate of turn in the last quarter if there is any appreciable wind. The aim should be a constant rate of turn at a constant height over a fixed position. RPM must, of course, be maintained throughout.

6. **Turns Around the Tail Rotor**

   These should be done in a training circle for real accuracy. The helicopter is flown sideways using the cyclic stick while your pedals are used to move the nose of the helicopter through 360 degrees thus describing a circle whose centre is the tail rotor. The fore and aft axis of the helicopter revolves like the spoke of a wheel. This turn is practised during this exercise as a precision manoeuvre. Rate of turn, height and position being accurately controlled.

7. **Airmanship**
   a) Lookout and tail clearance.
   b) Engine T's and P's.
   c) Wind velocity and helicopter limits.
   d) CG position.

you on this. However, as RRPM decays the tail rotor will become less effective therefore it may well be necessary to apply more right pedal in order to run on straight when using the lever to touch down.

5. **Altitude/Air Density**

At high altitudes or in conditions of high density altitude, the air is less dense than at sea level. Due to this reduced air density a higher pitch angle is required, assuming constant RPM, to maintain rotor thrust equal to weight. However, the kinetic energy of the blades remains constant. Therefore the control response of the lever is reduced and timing of the lever can, in certain conditions, become critical. An example of these conditions would be a hot mid-summer day with no wind.

6. **Airmanship**

Prior to the EOL, normal HASEL checks must be carried out downwind. When turning into wind for line-up, check that the area is clear of obstacles and aircraft and note the final wind velocity. In winds of less than ten knots ensure a ground speed run on of at least ten knots to maintain airflow over the disc. In winds of ten knots or more, a positive groundspeed is recommended for the basic student.

7. **Variable Flare Technique**

This technique is probably the most popular method of carrying out an EOL. Enter from 800 feet, eighty mph into normal sixty mph autorotation (in strong winds, higher airspeeds are recommended). Throttle back to 2,000 ERPM. Check rotor RPM,

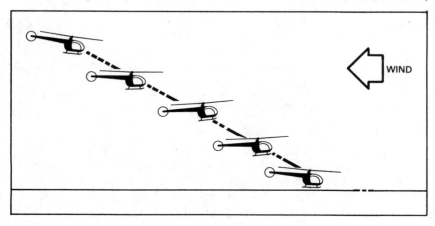

speed and height. When SURE of making the field close the throttle completely. Monitor the height, airspeed and RRPM and check the lever is fully down. At about seventy-five feet AGL gently raise the nose to reduce airspeed and rate of descent. At twelve to fifteen check with lever and level the helicopter for landing, ensuring that there is no drift. Cushion the touchdown with lever. Maintain a lookout ahead to ensure a straight run-on with pedals. When the helicopter comes to rest, lower the lever.

8. Constant Attitude Technique

The technique is as for the variable flare with two exceptions. Firstly the autorotation speed is forty mph and secondly, because of the low airspeed you definitely DO NOT FLARE. Cushion touchdown with one continuous movement of the lever at about twelve to fifteen feet, maintain a level attitude and run-on in the normal manner. It is most important to maintain forty mph so continuously scan and monitor the airspeed and be very wary of the effect on airspeed of any possible wind shear during the last 200 feet of the descent. DO NOT ATTEMPT TO RECOVER AIRSPEED BELOW 200 FEET.

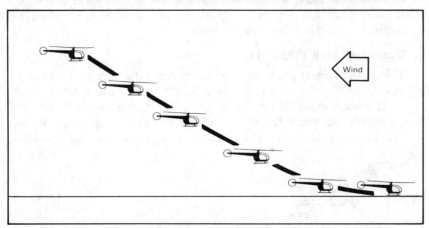

No-Flare Autorotation.

9. Crosswind and Downwind

In the event of finding yourself having to carry out an EOL crosswind, ensure there is no drift and run-on with at least ten knots of groundspeed. Downwind EOL's are not recommended but if such is your misfortune, then positive airspeed must be maintained and a high run-on speed accepted.

closing the throttle to prevent engine overspeed. However, to get maximum range benefit it is essential to ensure eighty mph airspeed from the outset. Once the lever is down, close the throttle to 2,000 ERPM and then check up slightly on the lever to reduce the RRPM. Only a small check is required but due to the lag from control movement to rotor response it is essential to wait a few seconds to check the RRPM. You may then adjust them if necessary with lever. At 200 feet above flare height (i.e. about 400 feet AGL), you must initiate a conversion to a sixty mph autorotation. To do this flare gently to the sixty mph attitude and lower the lever fully to regain RRPM. When settled you are ready to do either an engine-off landing or a normal recovery to the climb.

During a 360 or 180 degree turn, it is possible to overspeed the RRPM due to application of positive 'g' in the turn. To prevent this a small check up on the lever is required and as for the range auto, wait to see the effect of this on the RRPM before making a further adjustment. On rolling out of the turn remember to lower the lever again. During the turn the rate of descent will increase.

3. Airmanship

HASEL checks again, with special emphasis on lookout are essential. Do not throttle back below 2,000 ERPM. Check wind velocity. A verbal warning before each entry of 'Practice engine failure' is required to prevent any confusion between you and your instructor.

4. Conclusion

You will find this exercise most rewarding and the knowledge and skill gained from it is the basis for successful forced landings into fields of your choice. The importance of forced landings is no doubt already apparent to you.

Exercise 18   FORCED LANDINGS

1.   Introduction

The forced landing is the practical application of the advanced autorotation techniques taught in the previous exercise. By the end of the next few periods it will be within your capabilities to simulate an engine failure from 1,500 feet or so and make a safe autorotative approach to a landing site of your choice.

2.   Choice of Landing Area

The rapid consideration of several interrelated factors will decide your landing area or field for any particular situation. These are:

a)   Height above ground level. The higher the helicopter the greater the range over the ground. N.B. Do not attempt a 360 degree turn below 1,000 feet AGL or a 180 degree turn below 700 feet AGL. You should always aim to have the helicopter rolled out straight from a turn by 300 feet whether or not you have made it into wind.

b)   Wind direction and strength. The stronger the wind the less range into wind. Wind direction will determine the autorotative pattern.

c)   Distance to field. Is it within the autorotative capabilities of the helicopter to reach the field?

d)   Obstacles. Cables, high trees, buildings, etc. on the final approach.

e)   Surface. Green fields are preferred to ploughed or rocky surfaces.

f)   Size. A small football field is the ideal minimum.

3.   Basic Autorotative Patterns

Work out for yourself the basic patterns that might be employed in order to reach a suitable landing site after an engine failure. There are many possibilities and the best pattern to be employed for a forced landing can only be decided by weighing up the various merits of all the factors. It must be emphasized that the wind direction is not of paramount importance necessarily, although its effect on the planning of the autorotative pattern will be greater as the wind speed increases.

Consider these situations:

a) Helicopter into wind:
    Possible landing areas lie within a sector extending ahead and either side up to a limit of a range auto.

b) Helicopter downwind:
    Providing the helicopter is at or above 700 feet AGL, a 180 degree turn is feasible.

If plenty of height is available, it may be preferable to continue downwind in autorotation for a short time before making the 180 degree turn into wind.

c) Helicopter with crosswind from left:
    An 's' turn could be employed to lose height without covering too much distance over the ground.
    Avoid a 270 degree turn into wind because the pilot sitting in the left hand seat would not be able to keep the potential landing area in sight during the right hand turn.

d) Helicopter with crosswind from right:
    If height permits turn into wind. This should be carried out as quickly as possible in order that the left hand seat pilot can start choosing a landing site without delay. Embarrassing excess height could be lost with a left hand 270 degree turn.

4. Forced Landing Drill

You have had an engine failure and entered autorotation. You have also set-up a pattern for your pre-selected field. It is important for you to send out a Mayday call and to complete some vital actions before making an engine-off landing. These would be as follows:

a) MAYDAY, MAYDAY, MAYDAY: C/S, C/S, C/S: nature of distress, intentions, position. The earlier the call is made the more chance it has of being heard. Do not let the call interfere with your flying but do attempt to get some sort of distress call out no matter how abbreviated.

b) Assess cause of failure if time permits – do not attempt to restart below 800 feet AGL.

c) Mixture to idle cut-off, magneto's and generator OFF, check harness locked and tight, also check passengers. Battery OFF when finished with radio.

REMEMBER THAT TOP PRIORITY IS TO REACH YOUR LANDING SITE.

5. **Overshoot Procedure (Away from the Airfield)**

To practise the forced landing procedure without an engine-off landing at the end of each approach, you must do the normal recovery to the climb and be climbing away by a minimum of 500 feet AGL. Re-engagement after a normal autorotation will be done from 700 feet AGL. After a range autorotation, recover to a normal sixty mph autorotation at 800 feet AGL.

6. **Airmanship**

Finally, the airmanship for forced landing practices:

a) Normal HASEL checks and w/v.

b) Do not throttle back below 2,000 ERPM.

c) Clear the area underneath the helicopter and look out for obstacles on the approach to the intended landing site.

d) Do not descend below 500 feet on the recovery.

Exercise 19   STEEP TURNS

1. **Airmanship   HASEL Checks**

    Steep turns are purely an extension of medium rate turns flown at eighty mph and forty-five degree bank. The reduction of speed means more power available to keep the helicopter in a sustained turn.

    a) **Lookout.** Due to the fast rate of change of direction a good lookout before turning is essential. During the turn lookout should be maintained.

    b) **Technique.** Roll into the turn smoothly with cyclic, judging the angle of bank from where the rotor disc intersects the horizon.

    Maintain height with lever, RPM with throttle, airspeed with cyclic and balance with pedals.

    c) **Orientation.** After a number of consecutive steep turns it is possible to become disorientated. Keep a periodic check of your position.

    d) **Controls.** It is easy to misuse the controls during a steep turn, in particular trying to maintain height with the cyclic stick.

    This of course should only be used to maintain airspeed as in normal level flight. It is also common to fly out of balance during the turn. Cross check with the ball occasionally and correct any yaw.

    e) **Disc Loading.** Disc loading is increased during a steep turn and increase in RPM should be checked.

    With practice a high degree of accuracy can be achieved when flying steep turns.

Exercise 20   PRECISION TRANSITIONS

1.   Introduction

This is essentially an advanced co-ordination exercise aimed to increase confidence when manoeuvring close to the ground at higher than normal speed. The exercise consists of a transition from the hover to forward flight and back to the hover whilst maintaining constant height and heading.

2.   Airmanship

As the exercise involves the use of a large part of the airfield it is important to keep a lookout very carefully and ensure that you are not going to upset another aircraft's exercise. Bearing in mind that a high power setting is being used for most of the time it is essential to scan the engine instruments and maintain RPM within the prescribed limits.

In the initial stages of the transition power is needed to compensate for the loss of ground effect. As speed increases further translational lift is gained, usually signalled by a slight airframe shudder and a sudden indication of airspeed. Power has therefore to be reduced to maintain constant height. Throughout the accelerative phase it is necessary to compensate for the effects of disc flapback by moving the cyclic forward to maintain the accelerative attitude. Speed should be stabilized at sixty mph for a short period. To slow down again, a slight decelerated attitude is selected and the lever lowered to maintain a constant height. As the helicopter slows down translational lift is lost and the lever has to be raised again to prevent loss of height. The disc will flap forward as speed reduces so a small backward movement of the cyclic is necessary to maintain the decelerative attitude. As speed approaches zero the hover attitude is selected and the helicopter brought to a gentle stop. Flying RPM are maintained throughout and heading controlled with the pedals.

Exercise 21   QUICK STOPS, DOWNWIND EMERGENCY TURNS

1. Introduction

The quick stop is intended more as an exercise in co-ordination of the controls than an attempt to come to the hover in the minimum distance. The applications of the quick stop are when low flying either on survey or agricultural work or when forced to fly low because of poor weather conditions.

2. Quick Stop

a) **Entry.** The first few quick stops will be entered at a low airspeed so that the flare effects and control movements will be reasonably small. As co-ordination is acquired the entry speed will be progressively increased. During the quick stop the object is to maintain height (thirty feet approximately), direction (into wind), and RPM, until the hover is established. The quick stop is entered by gently flaring the helicopter and lowering the lever smoothly to prevent the helicopter climbing. This will cause the RPM to rise and this must be controlled with the throttle. Right pedal should be applied as required to prevent the helicopter from yawing.

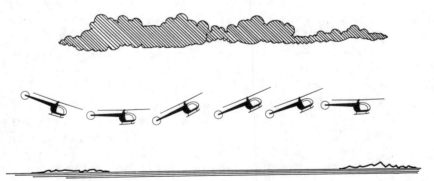

b) **Recovery to the hover.** As soon as the helicopter is flared, it will start to decelerate. As airspeed is reduced so translational lift is reduced resulting in a considerable loss in rotor thrust as the helicopter approaches the hover. Power must be applied, therefore, to maintain height as speed decreases through approximately forty mph and it must be applied at an ever increasing rate until the hover is established. Remember that more power is required to hover outside ground effect than to fly at eighty mph. To maintain direction with such a large increase in power progressive use of left pedal is required. Also, to maintain a nose-up attitude, rearward cyclic will be required to counter flap forward as speed decreases. Just before the groundspeed reaches zero select the hover attitude and establish a high hover. Gently descend vertically to a normal hover height.

3. Vortex Ring

As you approach the hover, you have two of the three conditions required for vortex ring, i.e. low forward speed and power inducing a flow through the rotor. If at this point, you let the helicopter descend then there is a likelihood of vortex ring state.

4. Downwind Emergency Turn

The downwind emergency turn is simply a level steep turn of forty-five degree bank from a downwind or crosswind position into wind. Once a balanced steep turn has been initiated, speed can be lost by raising the nose. If this is done the lever must be lowered to prevent climbing and right pedal used to remain in balance. Airspeed must be maintained over twenty mph until the helicopter can either be brought to the hover with a quick stop into wind or accelerated into normal cruising flight.

The steep turn is the normal evasive manoeuvre when low flying if you are unable to go over an obstacle due to weather reasons. Once the obstacles has been avoided then the desired track can be resumed.

Alternatively, if the lateral space available to turn is limited, the helicopter may be flared first and then rolled into a balanced turn towards the wind. Once again assuring the twenty mph is maintained until within thirty degrees of the wind heading.

Exercise 22 PILOT NAVIGATION

1. **Introduction**

   The object of this exercise is to introduce you to the environment associated with navigating a helicopter. A revision of the following points will be given.

   a) Significance and application of meteorological forecasts.

   b) Computation of headings, groundspeeds, safety heights and ETA's. Nature of terrain.

   c) Selection and preparation of maps.

   d) Methods of correcting headings and ETA's.

   e) Use of radio aids.

   f) ATC regulations, notams, and other airspace restrictions.

   g) Lost procedure.

   h) Diversions.

   i) Range and endurance flying.

   Initially some difficulty will be experienced in flying the helicopter accurately and map reading simultaneously. Also, orientation problems may occur because of the large drift angles that may be experienced.

2. **Airmanship**

   Do not let your concern for navigational detail override normal airmanship requirements.

2. **Setting Heading**

   A general check on initial heading should be made by reference to local features in order to detect any large error at once.

4. **Map Reading**

   a) Pinpoints depend on their unique qualities in terms of their surroundings for their value and reliability. The value of some pinpoints may change with seasonal or weather conditions.

   b) Don't get confused by trying to map read in too much detail, concentrate on major pinpoints in conjunction with the flight plan.

5. In Transit

Check fuel contents and consumption at planned check points. T's and P's must be regularly checked.

6. Use of Radio Aids

All bearings should be carefully checked, especially if they indicate the need for a large change in flight plan.

7. Low Level Navigation

At low level, the quality of pinpoints may change, with more emphasis on height and outline than on plan view. Small but unique features may be of more use at low level than the larger more common variety. Features can easily be missed, particularly if they are visible for only a short time, therefore, learn to anticipate check points. Careful pre-flight study of the map will be of use here. If one check point is missed continue with the flight and anticipate the next feature. If a succession of check points fail to materialize climb to a safe height and take steps to establish your position.

a) Check heading flown, time since last pinpoint, and establish circle of uncertainty.

b) Consider the effects of weather, e.g. rain on the canopy, areas of turbulence.

c) Consider the effects of sun and shadow, dazzle concealment of cables and other obstacles.

d) Remember the relatively slow speed of the helicopter and the considerable effect of wind.

e) At low level the wind will be affected considerably by terrain and large errors will occur if a constant check is not kept on the wind.

If you are still uncertain of your position, either:

a) Backtrack to last known location.

or

b) Fly to the nearest major line feature and fly along it reading ground to map to identify your position.

DO NOT WANDER AROUND AIMLESSLY.

Exercise 23   OUT OF WIND MANOEUVRES

1. Introduction

Helicopters are sometimes required to take-off, transition to the climb, approach and land out of wind. The procedures you will learn in this exercise will enable you to cope with all of these conditions.

2. Airmanship

Check heater is off. Maximum crosswind and downwind component twenty mph.

3. Take-off and Landing Out of Wind

You will already be familiar with the effects of hovering out of wind. From an accurate hover lower the helicopter gently onto the ground. After the skids touch, continue to hold the cyclic stick into wind to avoid slipping sideways along the ground. On take-off, position the cyclic into the wind to avoid drifting sideways.

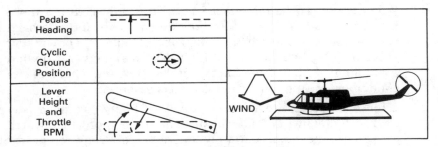

Crosswind Take-off.

Crosswind Landing.

4. Downwind Transitions

Downwind transitions should normally be avoided but this is not always possible. As soon as the helicopter moves away downwind AIRSPEED decreases as GROUNDSPEED increases, when GROUNDSPEED is the same as WINDSPEED, the helicopter is effectively flying in a no-wind condition. To maintain height at this stage a significant increase in power is required over the original hover power setting. To continue to accelerate downwind even more power is required (as in a normal transition) until translational lift is obtained. Note again that groundspeed is greater than the airspeed reached.

a) **Cushion Transitions.** From a low hover move gently forwards increasing power progressively. Keep close to the ground ensuring that maximum climb power is applied. Note that the gain in airspeed is much lower than the gain in groundspeed. Climb away when climbing speed is achieved using the speed for best ANGLE of climb if obstacles have to be cleared.

b) **Towering Transitions.** If the ground is unsuitable for cushion transitions and providing the power available is sufficient, a towering transition may be carried out. From a low hover apply maximum power available and climb vertically to a safe height. Before the rate of vertical climb starts to reduce ease forward into forward flight aiming to avoid a loss of height. Note the gain of groundspeed compared with airspeed. Climb away as in paragraph a).

c) Once obstacles have been cleared normal climbing speed can be resumed; a turn into wind will improve the angle of climb.

5. Downwind Approaches

When landing on a mountain site or in a tight clearing there may be occasions when a carefully flown downwind approach is safer than any other. In variable wind conditions a downwind approach may be made unwittingly. The maximum downwind component is small – ten knots – and so a careful check of site conditions, escape routes and C of G is essential.

Choose a landing site and fly a circuit at about 500 feet so as to approach downwind. Make a constant angle approach – watch air and groundspeeds carefully and anticipate required power changes. Keep control movements to a minimum and aim to keep an ample power margin in hand at all times. Bring the helicopter to a low hover and land.

An overshoot is mandatory if:

a) Directional control becomes difficult or the stick approaches the aft limit. These symptoms indicate that the tailwind component is excessive.

b) Power is within 2″ of maximum available MP.

c) Rate of descent is too high.

Exercise 24 SLOPING GROUND LANDINGS

1. Introduction

The technique of landing on sloping ground has been devised to cater for the worst conditions. The whole essence of the technique is gentleness and precise control to ensure that the helicopter does not roll over or slide out of control if the ground proves to be very bad. Do not land down-slope and be aware of the superimposed effect of the wind when choosing landing direction.

2. Landing

After a careful inspection of the site come to an accurate hover and check w/v, T's and P's, control position, C of G and that the heater 'off'. Lower the lever **very slowly** maintaining position accurately with cyclic stick and pedals. Ensure that the skid nearest the ground touches gently. If not, take off and try again. When this skid is in contact with the ground continue to lower the lever extremely carefully. As this is being done, move the cyclic stick to maintain disc position roughly parallel to the horizon. Ensure that the remaining skid touches lightly and continue to lower the lever until both skids are firmly on the ground and the lever is fully down.

If the blade or cyclic stops are encountered or the ground is suspect, take off and try again. If the ground is known to be firm and the slope appears acceptable and the second skid is nearly down when the stops are met, move the cyclic stick slowly towards the centre and at the same time continue to lower the lever until the helicopter is firmly down or it is apparent that a safe landing is out of the question.

In NIL WIND CONDITIONS the best landing positions are:

1st Right skid up slope.

2nd Nose up slope.

3rd Left skid up slope.

3. Taking Off

The same amount of caution should be used during take-off as during landing. Ensure that the disc is horizontal then gently raise the lever, moving the cyclic stick towards the centre to maintain the disc position. When the helicopter is in the hovering attitude lift it smoothly and positively clear of the ground.

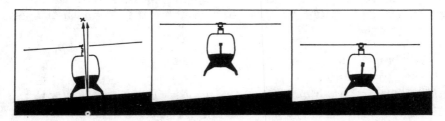

4. Airmanship

a) Never turn the tail towards the slope.

b) Maintain flying RPM at all times in case it is necessary to take-off rapidly.

c) Never land facing down the slope.

5. Limitations

a) Solo students are not permitted to land or take-off on sloping ground with a downwind component.

b) Sloping ground landings left skid up slope – Dual only basic stage, dual/solo in advanced stage.

c) With right skid up slope and crosswind from right – Dual and solo in advanced stage.

Exercise 25   LIMITED POWER OPERATIONS

1. Introduction

Under certain ambient conditions the power margin available may be limited and special techniques must be used for take-offs and landings. To practice these techniques your instructor will restrict the engine manifold pressure to an appropriate figure for simulation. It must be stressed that the techniques you will be taught must not be employed to fly the helicopter above MAX. AUW.

2. Power Checks

In conditions where the power margin is limited, e.g. in hot climates or high altitudes, it is essential that you know the margin between power available and power required before you commit your helicopter to a landing or take off. This can be achieved by two set procedures, the pre-landing and pre-take-off power checks. These are set out below and from a table of pre-determined results the capabilities of the helicopter can be calculated.

Landing Power Checks. Fly at forty mph and note the Manifold pressure required to maintain level flight. Increase power to check that maximum permissible Manifold Pressure can be obtained. The power margin available is the difference between the two figures obtained. The landing capabilities of the helicopter are set out below

a) Less than 2″ of Manifold Pressure in hand.   –   a run-on landing is necessary.

b) 2″–4″ of Manifold Pressure in hand.   –   a '0' speed landing is possible.

c) 5″ of Manifold Pressure in hand.   –   a 2ft hover is possible.

d) 6″ of Manifold Pressure in hand.   –   a 4ft hover is possible.

e) 7″–8″ of Manifold Pressure in hand.   –   a steep transition to 4ft hover is possible.

The power check must be flown in smooth conditions and care should be taken against false readings due to turbulence. It should be completed at a safe height near the proposed landing site.

Other factors will also influence the approach and landing techniques you will choose, but these will be covered in detail.

Committal Height. At some point on the approach a height will be reached below which it would be dangerous to overshoot. This height will depend not only on power available but on the highest obstruction on the approach and overshoot path, the nature of the landing area and the wind and turbulence encountered. Normally at least 2″ of power must be kept in hand and translational lift maintained down to the committal height in any approach. When practicing with simulated limited power conditions a committal height is unnecessary but for simulation a height of 100 feet is chosen as the decision point.

Take-Off Power Check. Establish to steady 2ft hover and note manifold pressure reading. The maximum power available will be the maximum permissible or obtainable manifold pressure. The various types of take-off and transition techniques and their governing power margins are set out below:

a) Less than 1″ of Manifold Pressure in hand. – a running take-off is necessary.

b) 1″–2″ of Manifold Pressure in hand. – a cushion creep take-off can be achieved.

c) 2″–5″ of Manifold Pressure in hand. – a towering take-off can be achieved.

d) 5″+ of Manifold Pressure in hand. – a vertical climb OGE can be achieved.

3. **Take-Off Techniques**

Th various types of take-off and transition techniques are outlined briefly below.

a) **Running Take-Off.** Ensure that the take-off and climb path is flat and clear of obstacles. The best method of executing a running take-off is to raise the lever to apply maximum available power and gently move the cyclic forward to achieve acceleration. As the speed increases allow the helicopter to fly off. Care must be exercised as the helicopter breaks contact with the ground as there is a nose pitch-down tendency and this must be counteracted with cyclic control. The angle of climb achieved will be very shallow, especially in slack wind conditions. The speed to give the best angle of climb is forty mph.

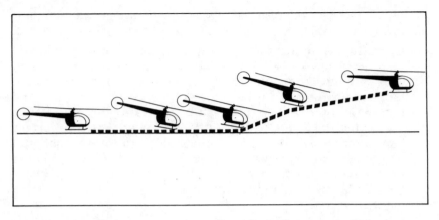

b) **Cushion Take-Off.** Ensure that the take-off and transition path is suitable for exploiting the ground effect of the rotor downwash, i.e. reasonably flat and clear of obstructions. From a steady hover accelerate gently forward, being careful to maintain a low, safe height over the ground. The acceleration will be slow until translational lift speed is reached when a gentle climb can be commenced as in a) above.

c) **Towering Take-Off.** From a low hover apply maximum power and let the helicopter climb vertically. **Before** the vertical rate of climb begins to fall off ease the cyclic gently forward so that translational lift will replace ground effect and forward flight maintained. The climb should be gauged in relation to the obstacles to be cleared. Towering take-offs require smooth flying and an accurate assessment of power margins. The dangers of misjudgment are obvious. IF YOU HAVE ANY DOUBTS ABOUT A TOWERING TAKE-OFF . . . DON'T!

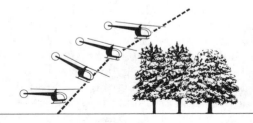

d) **Vertical Climb.** With 5″ or more in hand it should be possible to climb vertically out of the ground effect. It will be difficult to maintain a true vertical climb, so pick markers in front and to the side to help in maintaining ground position. During the descent beware of vortex ring state and be careful not to overpitch.

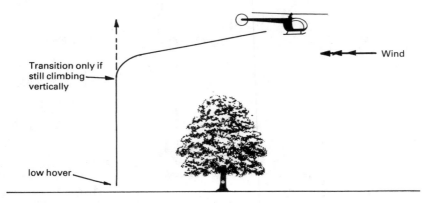

4. **Landing Techniques**

a) **Zero Speed and Run-On Landings.** With a power margin of 4" MP in hand it should be possible to effect a hover a few inches above the ground providing a gradual transition in the ground cushion can be made. This does not allow for any manoeuvre margin and thus it is safer to execute a zero speed landing without a hover. If the power margin is less than 4" MP a run-on landing may be necessary, the minimum touchdown speed being governed by the amount of power in hand.

   i) An inspection of the landing area should be made to ensure that it is suitable. During the inspection select a committal height below which it would be dangerous to attempt an overshoot with less than 2" MP in hand. Very flat approaches should be avoided.

   ii) For a zero speed landing fly a circuit 500 ft above touchdown height. Carry out power and downwind checks. Maintain translational lift and 2" MP in hand on the approach until committal height is reached. Once committed, continue to reduce airspeed and height together using all available power. Ideally, touchdown should be achieved with zero groundspeed and full power applied.

iii) For a run-on landing the same approach is flown, but the helicopter must be allowed to touch down as maximum power available is reached accepting the groundspeed pertaining at the time.

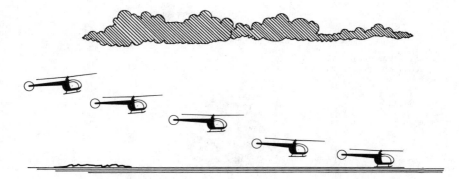

b) **2ft and 4ft Hover.** On this approach the pilot must closely co-ordinate power, speed and height from an accurate constant angle approach and he should aim to approach the hover point making best use of ground effect to compensate for loss of translational lift. A landing can then be made from a steady hover.

c) **Hover OGE.** This is attempted when no assistance can be expected from any ground effect, e.g. above trees. The last part of the approach to the hover point should be level and approximately ten feet above ground level or obstructions. Power and speed must be carefully co-ordinated, power increasing as speed falls off. Once the hover has been

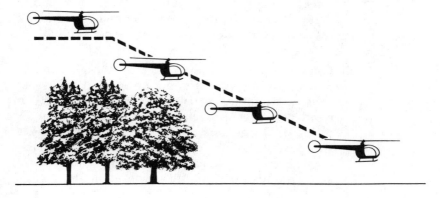

established, gentle manoeuvring may be permitted. Hovering should not be attempted above obstructions unless a vertical climb away can be achieved. For this reason 2″ MP is held in reserve, i.e. 7″ to achieve hover OGE + 2″ in reserve.

d) Very Steep Approach (7″–8″). On a very steep approach forward speed is low and therefore high power is required to prevent an excessive rate of descent. Translational lift may be lost before ground effect becomes apparent. For this reason an addition must be made to the power margin which, dependent on conditions, could bring it as high as that required for the hover OGE.

Exercise 26   CONFINED AREA OPERATIONS

1.   Introduction

In this exercise the basic techniques of operating in confined areas are demonstrated and practised. These techniques may be modified according to operational requirements and may be improved upon as experience is gained, however, a thorough knowledge of them at this basic stage is essential for safe operation.

It is important to remember that confined areas are not always surrounded by trees and that you may be called upon to operate out of areas surrounded by buildings. The basic operating techniques will still apply.

This exercise is closely allied to Limited Power (Ex 24) and various limited power techniques will be employed in confined area operations.

2.   Approaching the Confined Area Location

Before entering the confined area, or even deciding on the approach direction, it is important to check the power margin available. The forty mph power check is carried out in the vicinity of the landing site, preferably into wind at 500 feet AGL. For the purposes of this exercise, sufficient power for a high hover (6″ at least) is required before entering the area.

3.   Reconnaissance

Having established the power margin and identified the confined area accurately, the helicopter is flown over the landing site to check the following points:

a) Wind speed and direction.

b) General layout of the area; safe circuit direction, clear of obstacles if possible; identifying features close to the landing site to assist location of it when flying at low level. Check the height of the site.

c) Having assessed the wind velocity and general site layout, select the best approach path, escape route and exit path.

d) Select ground features ot identify the circuit turning points and any features that may assist in lining up on the approach.

e) Of the landing site itself check the size, shape, slope, surface, condition of the ground and any obstacles in the clearing. Select lateral markers to ensure safe tail clearance when descending into the site; also the intended hover point, ground effect and aiming point of the approach.

f) Select the Committal Height.

A 'High Recce' can be flown at a height of about 500 feet above the site at between fifty and sixty mph and serves to check the clearing layout, wind direction and to select the approximate approach direction and circuit pattern. A low recce is flown in the form of a circuit, a dummy approach and overshoot so that a closer look at the clearing is obtained.

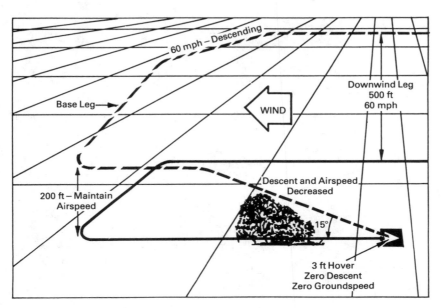

4. Circuit

The low level circuit is flown at 500 feet above the highest obstacle at fifty to fifty-five mph. A circuit utilizing identifiable turning points as well as prominent features selected around the landing site and on the approach path, enables the clearing to be kept identified throughout. Complete the normal circuit checks and maintain height and speed until the base leg.

5. Approach

Reduce airspeed on the base leg to give an initial groundspeed on the final approach of about forty mph. Height may also be reduced on the base leg or may be maintained depending on the nature of the obstacles. On the approach run-in, maintain height and speed until the desired sight picture is achieved. The angle of the approach will vary with the size of the clearing and the height of the obstacles as well as the wind conditions and power margin.

There are three main variations:

a) **Constant Angle.** The ideal approach if the site is large enough.

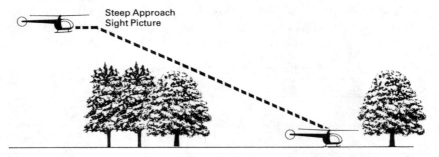

b) **Double-Angle Approach.** When a single angle approach would be unacceptably steep a shallow approach is made

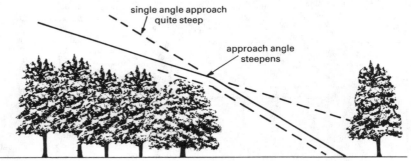

until the hover point becomes visible and then converted to a steep approach. Used in smaller clearings or when obstacles are high.

c) **Vertical Final Approach.** Used in small, deep, confined areas and is a progression from the double-angle approach.

During the approach smooth flying and careful co-ordination are essential as the power margin may be small.

The initial approach is flown as a dummy or trial approach if there is any uncertainty as to the condition along the approach or the power margin available. In this case the helicopter is levelled off at committal height and flown across the landing site at a minimum airspeed of twenty mph before overshooting. This dummy approach serves to check the existence and strength of any turbulence or wind shear on the approach and enables a close recce of the landing site to be made.

Over-shooting. It is mandatory to overshoot on the approach before committal height is reached if the power used gives less than 2″ of manifold pressure in reserve or an excessive rate of descent and low airspeed exist. Once below committal height the approach must be continued.

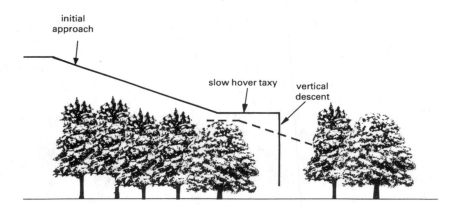

6. **In the Clearing**

The approach is made to a high hover (six to eight feet) over the landing point, taking care not to move forward into the trees and induce overhanging branches into the disc. The high hover ensures clearance above obstacles and tall undergrowth on the floor of the site. Power required may be very close to the maximum limit in this situation so careful handling is essential.

The Clearing Turns. Before the landing is carried out it is essential to manoeuvre the helicopter around the clearing to select the best landing spot and to familiarize yourself with the layout of the site. Two types of turns are practised in this exercise:

a) **Turn about the tail rotor.** Maintaining a high hover with the tail rotor in a clear area, the helicopter is turned about the tail rotor to the left keeping the disc well clear of the trees and obstacles in front of the helicopter.

b) **Sideways manoeuvring.** If the clearing is quite large the helicopter can be flown sideways for a distance equivalent to the length of the helicopter. Having 'cleared' that area, the helicopter is turned ninety degrees to the left about the pilot's position and the manoeuvre repeated until the whole clearing has been inspected.

Landing. The actual touchdown in the clearing, either on hard-standing or on open ground, is treated as a sloping ground landing. Avoid tail up the slope landings.

7. Leaving the Confined Area

A safe exit from the confined area depends largely on a good power margin for either a towering type take-off or vertical climb and a carefully selected exit route. Firstly, select your exit route. This entails manoeuvering about the clearing and selecting a low area in the surrounding obstructions, if possible into wind, although a small out-of-wind situation is acceptable. If power is expected to be limited, position the helicopter so as to make best use of the length of the clearing.

Come to a low hover, avoid obstructions, carry out the power checks and establish the power margin. If there is any doubt as to the performance of the helicopter, a trial vertical climb is carried out to see if it is possible to get above the obstructions before moving forwards.

If the length of the clearing is sufficient the transition from the towering take-off may be carried out just below the height of the obstructions ahead. However, this requires considerable judgement and should only be attempted after considerable experience is gained. Not a solo technique at this stage.

Before leaving the clearing, check above to ensure that there are no overhanging branches on adjacent trees that could become entangled with the main rotor. The forty mph best angle of climb speed is used until the helicopter is well clear of obstacles.

Exercise 27   INSTRUMENT FLYING

1. Introduction

It is sometimes required that helicopter pilots have to operate in adverse weather conditions and at night. Regular training and practice must be carried out to reach and maintain a satisfactory standard. The instrument flying exercises flown are designed to introduce you to the techniques involved and as a prelude to night flying.

The helicopter is basically unstable and you will find instrument flying extremely tiring in the early stages.

During the previous lessons you have seen how the instrument indications have tied up with actual helicopter movement but you have used mainly external references to establish and maintain a flight condition. However, when flying on instruments alone any deviation from the required flight condition must be picked up purely from instrument indications. Because of the lags and errors of certain instruments any change in flight condition will not be immediately indicated. To see any change in condition and correct as quickly as possible a regular scan must be established.

The primary instrument used in helicopter instrument flying is the artificial horizon or attitude indicator. Your scan must centre on this but should also include the ASI, altimeter, RCDI, directional gyro, slip indicator and tachometer. However, during a particular manoeuvre more time should be spent checking the instrument that will give immediate indications as to whether the manoeuvre is being executed correctly. Any tendency to disbelieve the instrument indications and rely on personal senses must be resisted. Secondary instrumentation must be checked at odd periods.

As you will have appreciated by now, some lag is incurred during changes of attitude. Failure to appreciate this while instrument flying will usually lead to overcontrolling and inaccurate handling.

2. Instrument Take-Off

If it is necessary to take-off and go into IMC immediately a special technique must be used. The helicopter is climbed vertically at full power, facing into wind, until a positive climb is indicated on the altimeter. The helicopter is then gently eased into forward flight ensuring that a rate of climb is maintained. Using this method the helicopter will avoid obstructions and avoid striking the ground, thus allowing the pilot to concentrate fully on instruments from an early stage.

3. Autorotations and Forced Landings

If an engine failure occurs under IMC, a procedure must be adopted that will give you the best chance of completing a safe landing. The helicopter is turned into wind and the normal daytime procedures completed. In an actual emergency the ground might not be seen until the last moment before impact. Therefore, to avoid the necessity for flaring, a constant attitude autorotation is established at forty mph when into wind. If the helicopter clears cloud before reaching ground level the speed can be adjusted as necessary to reach a safe landing area. Under simulated conditions an overshoot on instruments is completed from a safe recovery height.

4. Radio Aids

As you become more proficient you will begin to practice using radio aids. You will use VOR and ADF procedures as an introduction to more intensive instrument flying.

5. Unusual Attitudes

To recover from an unusual attitude use the following procedures:

a) Horizon level on artificial horizon.

b) Ball in the middle.

c) Control airspeed.

d) Adjust power for level flight.

7. Limits

a) Maximum height 10,000 feet.

b) Speed range 40–100 mph.

c) Maximum angle of bank 30 degrees.

Exercise 28   NIGHT FLYING

1.   Introduction

The night flying base is designed to introduce you to the special techniques required when operating a helicopter at night. The lessons flown will be confined to the circuit as the more practical applications will be introduced at a later date.

2.   Before Flight

As the lesson may be flown without the use of runway lights, taxiway lights and the approach aids it is essential that you fully understand the lighting systems and procedures in use before take-off.

3.   Airfield Lighting

a)   **Dispersal.** The helicopter dispersal will be illuminated by sodium lights, and the landing points by single glim lights.

b)   **Airfield Landing Point.** The airfield landing point will be marked by a standard 'T' as illustrated.

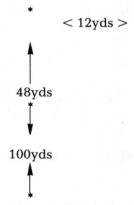

c)   **Line-up Lights.** to make lining up on the 'T' easier from the final turn, a small amber light is set out in front of the 'T' and in line with the tail of the 'T'. Another amber light is set out at the same distance above the head of the "T".

d)   **Autorotation Square.** A square is marked out on the airfield by amber lights for autorotation practice.

4.   Start-Up Procedure

On arrival at the aircraft the navigation lights are switched on and the landing lamp adjusted. Normal external checks are carried out with the aid of a torch.

On entering the cabin the interior lights are switched on.

When ready to start up, the navigation lights are switched off/on.

External power to be disconnected – flash navigation lights – no further ground crew assistance will be given.

To attract ground crew – flash landing lamp.

Ready for take-off – landing lamp on.

Running change-over – landing lamp off after touchdown.

5. **The Circuit**

   a) Full R/T is used at night for circuit flying. Calls are made for take-off, downwind, finals, downwind for autorotation, overshooting and entering and leaving the 'T'.

   b) The helicopter is air-taxied from dispersal, making use of the landing lamp.

   c) At the 'T' when permission has been received for take-off a towering transition technique is used. This is similar to the instrument take-off detailed in Exercise 26, and is used because of the loss of ground references and the possibility of disorientation during the early part of the take-off. Once a safe climb has been established a transfer to external references may be made.

   d) At night the circuit height is 1,000 feet. A descent to 500 feet is made on base leg.

   e) The approach flown at night is the same as that flown during the daytime. The correct approach angle is maintained by watching the apparent aspect of the 'T' and its position on the windshield.

   f) The approach is continued to the lead-in light, when the hover is established using the 'T' lights as a reference either left or right of the base light of the 'T'. When landing, 'T' lights should be used to avoid disorientation or drift on touchdown.

   g) If during the approach it becomes necessary to overshoot, call 'overshooting' and climb straight ahead.

   h) The flares are always armed and disarmed clear of the 'T' with the flare pointing in a safe direction.

6. Circuit Emergencies

a) Navigation light failure – inform ATC and continue circuit.

b) R/T failure – Continue circuit and R/T calls, receiver only may be unserviceable. Land as directed at local briefing.

c) Total electrics failure – Continue circuit at 800 feet using a torch to illuminate the instruments and land alongside main 'T'. Run down helicopter in normal way and switch off.

d) Engine failure – Use daytime procedure, establish a constant attitude autorotation, landing light on, and use Schermuly flares if fitted.

7. Airmanship

a) One torch to be carried in the cockpit.

b) Hover-taxi using the landing lamp and taxi in the direction of the light. Avoid taxying too fast and too high.

c) A good lookout at night is essential.

THE HELICOPTER NIGHT RATING

In order to fly as Pilot in Command (PIC) of a helicopter at night, with or without passengers, you must hold a Night Rating. The privileges are set out in Schedule 8 to the Air Navigation Order (ANO) 1989.

Before making an application for the rating you must have at least fifty hours as pilot of helicopters and have completed a recognised course of night flying instruction.

Before starting the night flying training you must have at least twenty hours as PIC of which ten hours must have been gained since your licence was issued and sufficient dual instruction in instrument flying of which not less than five hours must have been flown by sole reference to instruments. Up to 2.5 hours of this may be conducted in a simulator recognised by the Civil Aviation Authority (CAA) as being suitable for instrument training.

For the night training, you must complete a course of at least five hours night flying with and to the satisfaction of, a qualified helicopter instructor. The training shall consist of at least three hours dual instruction and include at least one night cross-country flight. Also, a minimum of five night flights as PIC each consisting of a take-off to the hover, transition into forward flight, climb to at least 500 feet, an approach and a landing.

The flights as PIC must have been obtained within the six months immediately preceding the date of your application for the night rating.

A helicopter Night Rating does not have to be revalidated, however, before carrying any passengers at night you must meet the night currency experience requirement. This states that at a time when the depression of the centre of the sun was not less than twelve degrees below the horizon, you have carried out at least five flights, each consisting of a take-off to the hover, transition into forward flight, a climb to 500 feet and a landing all as PIC and within the immediately preceding thirteen months.

HELICOPTER INSTRUMENT FLYING

The sphere of helicopter instrument flying is growing rapidly. With the introduction of better icing clearances and more sophisticated avionics, procedural instrument flying has now become a reality.

For your training, simulation of instrument flying conditions will be achieved by blanking off any window areas on your side of the helicopter and you wearing a visor to further restrict your peripheral vision.

It is important that you learn to **relax** during instrument flying. Before flight make sure that the seat and pedals are adjusted to give you maximum comfort. Remember that the basic techniques for instrument flying are exactly the same as for visual flight.

SCAN

Constant practice is required to achieve a regular and efficient scan together with gentle control movements.

The concept of the selective radial scan centres around the Artificial Horizon (AH), then to a second instrument, back to the AH, on to a third instrument, back to the AH and so on.

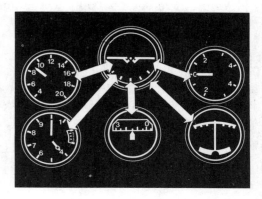

When carrying out any particular manoeuvre the scan should concentrate on the instruments relevant to that manoeuvre. It is wasted effort to include instruments which, at that stage of the flight, provide no useful information. For example, in a level turn the scan would follow the sequence — AH-VSI-AH-ASI-AH-COMPASS-AH-VSI etc. Note that the altimeter is not included in the scan since the VSI will give the first indication of a change in height. Should a change in height be detected then the altimeter must enter the scan sequence.

ATTITUDE CONTROL

During your initial flying training emphasis was placed on attitude flying. If a correction was required, the helicopter's attitude was adjusted against the visual horizon. When you fly on instruments the real horizon is no longer available and so the Artificial Horizon (AH) must be used instead. No basic change in technique is required; you simply use the AH in the same way that you see the real horizon in visual flight. Thus it is the primary instrument for selecting and determining the helicopter's attitude — the master flight instrument.

The pitch datum on the AH can be adjusted to be coincident with the horizon bar for any flight condition. Remember that any small attitude change shown on the AH will, if maintained, have a marked effect on the helicopter and therefore it is usual to set the datum against the central mark on the side scale and leave it there throughout the flight.

To avoid large attitude changes you must be extremely smooth on the cyclic and any changes must be small. Remember too that there is a lag in helicopter response so be patient and allow time for it to stabilize before making any further changes.

THE INSTRUMENT TAKE-OFF AND CLIMB

Your instructor will hover, taxy and position the helicopter for the instrument take-off because of the restricted visibility from your side.

The initial part of the instrument take-off is carried out visually. In the hover carry out normal hover checks and when ready initiate a 'towering type take-off'. Ensure the 'wings' are level, maintain compass heading and check balance. Confirm that the instrument indications agree with the visual facts and transfer to instrument flight by 100 feet agl.

Maintain the accelerative attitude and anticipate the attitude change to establish the best rate of climb speed for your particular helicopter. Adjust power, check balance and use bank if necessary to correct heading.

During the transition and climb the scan should follow between AH-ASI-AH-COMPASS-AH-BALANCE etc. Power should be included as necessary. The altimeter will assume greater importance as you approach your required height but apart from confirmation of serviceability, can be excluded in the early stages of the transition.

When levelling out from the climb, anticipate the height as normal and use the APT technique. If the helicopter is slightly off heading, check balance before applying any bank.

LEVEL FLIGHT AND SPEED CHANGES

Your instructor will show you level flight indications throughout the IF flight envelope for your type of helicopter. The important point to notice is that the speed stable attitude varies very little throughout the range.

The AH is used to select and maintain the attitude. The other instruments are used to monitor and confirm the helicopter's performance and are therefore referred to as PERFORMANCE instruments.

In level flight at a steady airspeed, the speed table attitude should be maintained. Initially, deviations from level flight will be indicated by the VSI; the altimeter in the helicopter suffers from large lag errors and takes some time to respond to height changes. If a rate of climb or descent is indicated refer to the AH, then the ASI. Make an appropriate small cyclic adjustment to correct the attitude, allow the helicopter to settle and then recheck. If a climb or descent is still indicated but airspeed is stable, adjust power and maintain balance.

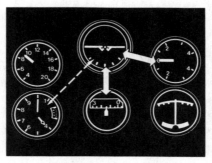

Maintaining S and L.

CLIMBING AND DESCENDING

During instrument flying you will be taught Procedural Climbing and Descending.

The technique is simply to maintain the cruise airspeed and adjust power to give 500 ft/min rate of climb/descent as required.

Climbing   *Descending*

Scan again centres on the selection and maintenance of the appropriate attitude on the AI, with cross reference to the power, VSI and ASI. Target heights should be anticipated by 10% of the rate of climb or descent.

TURNS

When flying on instruments, the normal angle of bank used is that which corresponds to a Rate 1 turn. To calculate the angle of bank required, the following rule of thumb can be used:

Note the airspeed

Ignore the units figure

Add 7 to the remaining figure = angle of bank required

For example: Airspeed 120 kts,
            ignore unit digit = 12,
            add 7 = 19,
therefore angle of bank required for a rate 1 turn at 120 kts is 19°.

For practical purposes you should use 10° of bank at 40 kts, 15° at 90 kts and 20° at 120 kts.

To enter a turn, first note the speed stable pitch attitude; smoothly and progressively apply the bank required whilst maintaining the pitch attitude. Anticipate the roll-out heading using the 'degree for degree' technique, e.g. if using 30° of bank, anticipate heading by 30°.

Entering a Turn   *Maintaining a Turn*

When carrying out climbing and descending turns on instruments always enter the climb or descent first and then apply the required amount of bank.

Descending Turn

ACTIONS IN THE EVENT OF SIMULATED EMERGENCY

An emergency involving an entry into autorotation and descending through cloud is obviously extremely hazardous. Apart from the cause of the emergency the greatest danger lies in descending through the Safety Height, in IMC conditions, into unknown terrain.

Entry into autorotation is exactly the same as for visual flight. Lower the collective lever fully, maintaining balance and select the Minimum Rate of Descent Speed.

Turn the shortest way into the last known or forecast wind and transmit a Mayday call. Carry out the appropriate drills for your type of helicopter. If you are still in cloud as you approach Safety Height, reduce speed as for Constant Attitude Autorotation. On breaking cloud (normally simulated at around 800 feet), transfer from instruments and complete the practice forced landing visually.

A less serious emergency is the loss of your alternator which will cause the gyros to slowly run down and become unreliable; in these circumstances they must be totally ignored. To avoid confusion and possible damage to the instrument, the AH should be caged if possible. Inform ATC of the problem.

There are other minor emergencies which may occur. Your instructor will discuss with you how being on instruments may modify your reactions to these emergencies. It is most important that you maintain your scan and not let the distraction of the emergency prevent you from retaining safe control of the helicopter.

RECOVERY FROM UNUSUAL ATTITUDES

It cannot be over-emphasized that you must trust your instrument indications implicitly. You must disregard any physiological sensations as they may well be giving you false information. Disbelief of the instruments can aggravate these sensations leading to disorientation which could then result in the helicopter entering an unusual attitude situation.

Your instructor will demonstrate these problems by manoeuvring the helicopter whilst you close your eyes or look away from the instruments. When you are then given control the objective is to quickly interpret the instrument information and smoothly recover to straight and level flight with a minimum loss of height.

Do not attempt to do too many things at once. The correct recovery actions, in order of priority are:

Refer to AH and level the 'wings'

Check balance (ball in the middle)

Check IAS:

If low — select an accelerative attitude and do not apply power until IAS is above thirty kts (Vortex Ring hazard)

If high — select a decelerative attitude and adjust power as necessary

Smoothly adjust attitude/power to achieve normal straight and level flight.

After you have completed the recovery subsequent actions are a matter of good airmanship, e.g. climbing back to a previously allocated altitude.

CONTROLLED DESCENT THROUGH CLOUD (QGH) PROCEDURE

In essence, this is a fairly simple procedure to bring you safely down through cloud so that you can complete your final approach and landing visually.

You will home overhead the airfield on height and heading instructions given by ATC and then be turned onto an Outbound Heading. This turn should be carried out at Rate 1 (180°/min).

The Outbound leg will be timed by ATC and you will then be instructed to turn onto an Inbound Heading — again a Rate 1 turn.

When steadily inbound, you will be cleared to descend to your approach minima. This descent should be carried out at 500 feet/min.

If you are still in cloud when you reach your approach minima you must abort the descent and carry out the Missed Approach Procedure.

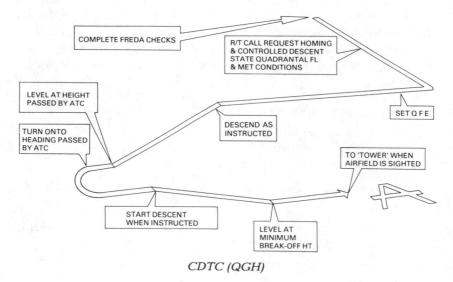

CDTC (QGH)

MISSED APPROACH PROCEDURE

This procedure combines the techniques of levelling off from a descent at a constant airspeed and those used for climbing.

Apply climb power, maintain a level attitude and control balance. You should now obey any missed approach instructions given by ATC.

RADAR APPROACHES

The two procedures most commonly used are the Surveillance Radar Approach (SRA) and Precision Approach Radar (PAR).

After your R/T request for the approach you will receive instructions and be guided into a radar approach procedure. This will position you at a safe height and distance from the instrument runway, from where you can be safely monitored throughout the descent.

On both types of approach, in still air, a 3° angle of approach will be achieved using a 400–500 feet/min rate of descent. Procedural rates of turn and descent are used throughout.

You must initiate a Missed Approach Procedure if you reach your approach minima without gaining visual references or if radar or R/T contact is lost.

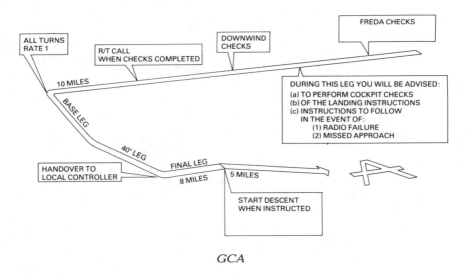

GCA

SUMMARY

The most common problems when you first begin your instrument training are likely to be:

Failure to fly attitudes

Overcontrolling, especially in the pitching plane, through 'chasing' the airspeed with the cyclic

Not maintaining a good, selective radial scan

So remember — FLY ATTITUDES, FLY SMOOTHLY AND SCAN.

HELICOPTER
NIGHT FLYING

You will find night flying a most enjoyable experience. It is usually smoother than by day because of the reduction of thermal or convection air currents. The handling of the helicopter is no different from day flying and the transition to night, particularly for the pilot trained in instrument flying, is quite straightforward.

The lights displayed by all aircraft at night not only indicate their presence to you but they can also be used to determine their position relative to yourself. For example, if you see a white light ahead you will know that you are astern of the other aircraft. If the white light changes into green, you will know that you are overtaking it on the starboard side or that he has turned to his right.

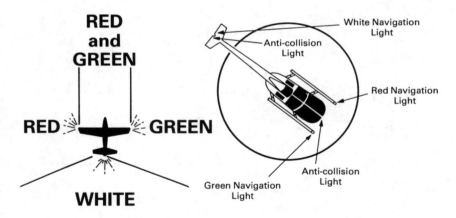

Much has been written about night vision, however, at our level of training all that is necessary is for us to walk out to the helicopter a little early and allow our eyes to adjust sufficiently themselves.

It takes the rods in the eye approximately thirty minutes to adjust themselves fully to night conditions but only a second or so to reverse the process! So be careful not to undo the effort by flashing a torch around — use the cabin lighting instead.

Airborne lookout at night is the same as for daytime. If you wish to look at an object, shift your gaze slightly off centre and do not hold a steady look for more than a few seconds. It is another characteristic of rod vision that an image fades completely if the eyes are kept stationary for more than a few seconds.

At night you will be using and operating services in the dark so it is good practice to spend some time in the helicopter before night flying begins learning their exact positions.

LIGHT SIGNALS

The following are the more usual light signals used to communicate your intentions to the groundcrew:

Ready to start engine — navigtion lights OFF/ON

Ready to engage rotor — anti-collision light ON

Call in groundcrew — flash your torch

Dismiss the groundcrew — landing lamp ON/OFF

TAKE-OFF AND HOVER TAXYING

Switch on your landing lamp and take-off to the hover. Do not stare into the pool of light but look well ahead and use the general all-round illumination. Hover taxy slightly higher than you would do in the daytime out to the take-off point.

Since night flying is a combination of instrument and visual flying it is important that the instruments are checked for serviceability whilst hover taxying out.

THE CIRCUIT

Note that all R/T calls for take-off are made from the hover so there is no need for a lookout turn. When cleared by ATC, carry out a towering type take-off and at about 300 feet, if it is safe to do so, switch your landing lamp off. Continue to climb straight ahead and level off at 1000 feet.

Drift appreciation diminishes at night and so the selection of heading/track references assumes greater importance.

Make the R/T call 'Downwind' when abeam the landing T to signify your wish to make a normal approach and landing. If your intention is other than this you must specify it in your call.

When you are established on final approach call 'Finals'. If the landing point is available ATC will clear you to land; if it is occupied you will be cleared to 'continue'.

The approach technique will depend on the type of landing aid in use. One rather basic but effective aid is the Proportional Flarepath.

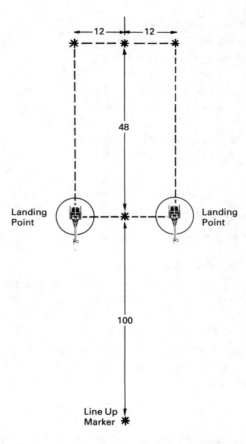

The aim here is to maintain a constant aspect throughout the descent. At about 300 feet switch on the landing lamp and continue the approach maintaining the aspect. Keep the helicopter moving in the hover taxy and establish the hover to one side of the landing point light.

GOING AROUND (OVERSHOOTING)

If for any reason you are not able to maintain a safe approach path or have not been given clearance to land by 200 feet, a go around (overshoot) must be initiated. As you commence the climb, turn at the same time 45° towards the circuit and call 'going around'. When you reach abeam the flarepath turn on to the circuit take-off heading and climb straight ahead to 1000 feet. If a go around is initiated below 200 feet, do not turn except to avoid overflying other helicopters.

INADVERTENTLY ENTERING CLOUD

If at any time you inadvertently enter cloud you must immediately go on to instruments and inform ATC. You may find the glare from the anti-collision lights disorientating, in which case switch them off until you are clear of cloud again.

PRACTICE AUTOROTATIONS

On the downwind leg carry out the HASEL checks and call 'downwind for autorotation'. Maintain height and speed on base leg and after turning on to final approach call 'finals for autorotation'.

On reaching a suitable point enter autorotation as normal. Once established, switch on the landing lamp and reduce airspeed to achieve a constant attitude landing technique.

Re-engage and initiate a go around by 200 feet, informing ATC.

EMERGENCIES

Emergencies at night are no different to those experienced by day. However, lighting and radio failures will cause particular problems, as does hydraulic failure.

Hydraulic Failure: Complete the normal drills and inform ATC. Make a normal angle of approach and touchdown at the landing point. Shutdown the engine but leave the navigation lights ON.

Cabin Light Failure: At the time of failure either use your torch or adjust the wander lamp to illuminate the instrument panel. Check that the instrument lights switch is set correctly. If the failure is confirmed, set the switch to OFF.

Navigation Light/Beacon Failure: You will normally be informed of these failures by ATC or by other helicopters. Check the switch and if the failure is confirmed set it to OFF. Complete the circuit and return to the parking area. Avoid other helicopters as they will be unable to see you.

Landing Lamp Failure: Inform ATC, switch the landing lamp OFF, continue with a careful approach, land and wait for further instructions.

Total Electrics Failure: Carry out any drills and continue the circuit using your torch. Remember that your radios will also have failed. Land at the touchdown point, shut down and try to attract the attention of ATC with your torch. Use your torch also to warn other helicopters and vehicles of your presence.

If the failure occurs when you are away from the circuit, rejoin carefully noting the position of other helicopters and land at the touchdown point.

Radio Failure: After confirmation of the failure, conform to the normal circuit pattern but slightly extending the downwind leg. On final approach, switch the landing lamp ON/OFF from about 500 feet at five second intervals. Leave it ON from 200 feet and continue down to the hover as normal. Turn towards the control tower and flash the landing lamp until you are answered with a 'green'. This clears you to return to the parking area.

NAVIGATION AT NIGHT

The pre-flight planning is the same as for daytime navigation. When studying your map consider the features which you think will be prominent at night, e.g. towns, motorways, etc. Obstruction lights and airfield identification beacons can be of use as are water features on moonlit nights.

Mark these selected features on your map so that they will show up under the cabin lighting.

The flight is conducted in a similar manner to a daytime navigation exercise. Divide your attention between events outside the helicopter and accurate flying/map study in the cabin.